On Reflection

On Reflection

Hilary Kornblith

OXFORD
UNIVERSITY PRESS

OXFORD
UNIVERSITY PRESS

Great Clarendon Street, Oxford, OX2 6DP,
United Kingdom

Oxford University Press is a department of the University of Oxford.
It furthers the University's objective of excellence in research, scholarship,
and education by publishing worldwide. Oxford is a registered trade mark of
Oxford University Press in the UK and in certain other countries

First Edition published in 2012

Impression: 1

British Library Cataloguing in Publication Data

Data available

Library of Congress Cataloging in Publication Data

Data available

ISBN 978–0–19–956300–5

Printed in Great Britain by
MPG Books Group, Bodmin and King's Lynn

To Ben

Acknowledgments

I've been working on the ideas in this book for quite some time. When I first moved to the University of Massachusetts in 2003, I put together a draft of a paper which eventually became 'What Reflective Endorsement Cannot Do'. I presented those ideas at quite a number of different department colloquia and conferences, rethinking and revising over the years. At some point during the process, it became clear to me that these ideas were worthy of extended development. I'm very grateful to the many audiences which provided so much input to the process.

Indeed, I've been very fortunate during this period to be able to try out my ideas in a great many different venues, providing me with stimulating reactions and provocations from very many people. A number of these occasions stand out. Thomas Grundmann invited me to conduct a week-long summer school in Cologne in 2007, and those extraordinarily intense sessions, lasting from early morning to late into the night, day after day, gave me a tremendous amount to think about. My final presentation of 'What Reflective Endorsement Cannot Do', at the Rutgers Epistemology Conference in 2007 was also especially productive. A conference in London in 2008 on Transcendental Philosophy and Naturalism allowed me to develop some of my ideas about the Pittsburgher Schule, and a ten-day stay in Hangzhou, China, in 2010 gave me a forum for trying out drafts of a few of the chapters of this book. A conference at UNAM in Mexico City in 2011, to celebrate Ernie Sosa's 70th birthday, allowed me to try out some of my ideas on epistemic agency. Finally, a visit to the University of Washington in 2011 allowed me to discuss some of these ideas at length with Larry BonJour and Bill Talbott. All of these occasions, and many others as well, have had a large impact on the final shape of this book.

I have also been very lucky over the years to have occasion to discuss these ideas with many friends who provided not only extremely useful comments and suggestions, but much encouragement as well. Larry BonJour, Jessica Brown, David Christensen, Alvin Goldman, Jennifer Lackey, Jennifer Nagel, Ram Neta, Derk Pereboom, Nishi Shah, Ernie Sosa, Jonathan Vogel, and Michael Williams have all been invaluable.

Amalia Amaya provided me with extended comments on my work on epistemic agency, as did Angeles Eraña. I have had the benefit of excellent graduate students here at UMass, and I have received especially helpful comments on pieces of this book from Kristoffer Ahlström and Alex Sarch. Most recently, a seminar on naturalism and the first-person perspective, which I have been teaching with Lynne Baker, has been wonderfully stimulating. Lynne thinks that the first-person perspective raises problems for naturalism; I think that naturalism raises problems for the first-person perspective. It's been great fun and terrifically illuminating to have the benefit of these weekly sessions with Lynne.

Peter Momtchiloff has been a fantastic editor, from his first discussion with me of these ideas up to the present moment. Two anonymous readers whom he obtained for the manuscript gave me wonderful comments, and they have resulted in a very large number of changes. I am very much in their debt.

I have published a number of papers which were incorporated into this book, although the ideas in the papers were typically extended, revised, and reorganized for their presentation here. Aside from 'What Reflective Endorsement Cannot Do', *Philosophy and Phenomenological Research*, 80 (2010), 1–19, I have also made use of work from the following papers: 'Sosa on Human and Animal Knowledge', in John Greco (ed.), *Sosa and his Critics* (Blackwell, 2004), 126–34; 'Replies to Alvin Goldman, Martin Kusch, and William Talbott', *Philosophy and Phenomenological Research*, 71 (2005), 427–41; 'Reply to Bermudez and BonJour', *Philosophical Studies*, 127 (2006), 337–49; 'The Metaphysical Status of Knowledge', *Philosophical Issues*, 17 (2007), 145–64; 'Sosa in Perspective', *Philosophical Studies*, 144 (2009), 127–36; and 'Reasons, Naturalism, and Transcendental Philosophy', in Joel Smith and Peter Sullivan (eds), *Transcendental Philosophy and Naturalism* (Oxford University Press, 2011), 96–119. I am grateful to the publishers of these volumes for permission to reprint this work here.

Contents

Introduction

Philosophers have valued reflection for as long as there has been such a thing as philosophy. Philosophy itself is a reflective activity, and so, perhaps, this should come as no surprise. It seems to me, however, that philosophers have typically assigned a great deal more value to reflection than it really deserves, and, more than this, they have done so because their view of what reflection is and what it is capable of achieving is terribly inaccurate.

I first became interested in the topic of reflection because of work I was doing in epistemology. The very idea of epistemological theorizing is often motivated in the following way. We typically arrive at our beliefs unreflectively, and when we do so, the processes by which our beliefs are produced are often quite unreliable. After all, we sometimes engage in wishful thinking; we form conclusions, at least at times, quite hastily and on the basis of remarkably little evidence; we are subject to errors and biases in our inferences. For these reasons, resting content with unreflective belief acquisition seems not only lazy, but irresponsible. Anyone who cares about having an accurate understanding of the world around us should thus stop to reflect, both on the beliefs he or she has, and on the reasons for which they are held. By holding one's beliefs up to reflective scrutiny in this way, we may substantially improve upon the accuracy of our beliefs. On some views, this sort of reflective scrutiny is held to be a necessary condition for having justified beliefs or knowledge.

This is, beyond doubt, an attractive picture, and it is terribly commonsensical. A certain problem is identified here at the first-order level—since unreflective belief acquisition runs the risk of unreliability—and second-order scrutiny is then introduced as the solution to the problem. But commonsensical as this picture is, there is something deeply wrong with it. Epistemologists are right to worry that first-order belief acquisition need not be reliable, even if, especially in presenting skeptical worries, the threat of unreliability is often exaggerated. But just as first-order processes of belief acquisition may not be uniformly reliable, we cannot simply assume that the processes involved in reflective scrutiny are themselves entirely reliable. Recognition of this fact raises two different problems for the simple picture sketched above.

First, if the possibility of unreliability can only be responsibly dealt with by way of higher-order reflection, then an infinite regress results. Our first-order beliefs cannot simply be assumed to be reliable, so we must reflect on them, their origins, and their logical relations, in order to assure ourselves that we have arrived at them as we should. But now the second-order beliefs produced by this reflective activity—the beliefs about our first-order beliefs, their origins, and their logical interrelations—cannot simply be assumed to be accurate or reliably produced either. And if in order to deal with this responsibly, we must engage in further reflection one level higher, then this will not provide a solution to our initial problem, but merely raise the same problem all over again at the third-order level. However much we may reflect, there will always be some level of belief which has gone unscrutinized. The demand that we reflect so as to avoid unscrutinized belief cannot ever be satisfied.

Serious as this is, however, it is not the only problem with our initial picture. Even if we cannot achieve the ideal of belief acquisition which has, in some sense, been fully vetted by reflection, we might still think that there is something fundamentally right about the idea that we should engage in at least some reflective scrutiny of our beliefs. The simple logical point about the infinite regress does nothing to undermine this suggestion. Surely we improve the quality of our belief acquisition by engaging in reflective scrutiny, even if, in the end, we must acknowledge that there will always be some level of belief acquisition which goes entirely un-scrutinized. Surely this much of the commonsense picture of the value of reflective scrutiny can be maintained. Or so it seems.

The problem with this idea, as it turns out, is not logical, but empirical. There is a great deal of work that has been done by social psychologists on the kinds of processes involved when we reflect on our beliefs, their origins, and their interrelations. To make a long story short,[1] these pro-cesses are a deeply mixed bag. Some of them are reliable, to be sure. But a

---

[1] I have told the longer story in *Knowledge and its Place in Nature* (Oxford University Press, 2002), ch. 4.

great many of these processes are terribly unreliable. In a very wide range of important cases, reflective scrutiny of our first-order beliefs does not allow us to recognize our errors and then correct them; instead, it gives us the misleading impression that first-order beliefs which are in fact mistaken and which were in fact arrived at in terribly unreliable ways, are perfectly accurate and were arrived at in a fully reliable manner. Engaging in reflection on our beliefs is thus proposed as a way of weeding out our errors and increasing our reliability, but in actual practice, it often succeeds in producing a far more confident, but no more reliable, agent. What commonsense tells us is a way of screening our beliefs in order to make them more accurate turns out, instead, in many cases, to be a route to little more than self-congratulation.

Once all of this became clear to me, I began to worry about the general form of this difficulty. A problem is presented at the first-order level, and reflection is brought in to provide its solution. But, at least as the problem is initially presented, reflection cannot possibly solve it. More than this, even the commonsense and more modest appeal to the value of reflection turns out to be problematic. The more I started thinking about this particular pattern, the more I saw it repeated in other areas of philosophy.

Thus, consider a question about reasons. What is involved in reasoning from premises to conclusion in an argument? Let us take an example. Suppose I believe that p and I also believe that if p, then q. Suppose as well that I now come to believe that q. What conditions must be met for my belief that q to have been arrived at on the basis of reasoning from my other two beliefs? One view has it that, in order for me to arrive at the belief that q on the basis of my other beliefs, I must have a certain higher-order belief: I must believe that my beliefs that p and if p, then q, together give me good reason to believe that q. On this view, forming beliefs on the basis of reasons requires forming explicit beliefs about those reasons. On some versions of this view, as we will see in Chapter 2 below, one must have such beliefs about reasons in order to have any beliefs at all.

Now just as we saw earlier with the view about the need for reflection if one is to have justified belief or knowledge, this particular view leads to an infinite regress. If in order to draw the conclusion that q from the given premises, I must also form the belief that my belief in the premises gives me good reason to believe the conclusion, we may now ask what relationship this new belief is thought to play in my reasoning. Quite clearly, it cannot simply be an idle bystander, for if it plays no role in my reasoning, then

I may have only been led to believe that q quite fortuitously. The whole point of insisting that I have this higher-order belief is to distinguish the cases in which I believe that q fortuitously from those in which I believe it on the basis of proper reasons. So the explicit belief about reasons must actually play an active role in my reasoning. But, at least according to this view, a belief can only play an active role in one's reasoning if one forms an explicit belief about that role. So now I need to form the belief that my belief that p, and my belief that if p then q, together with my belief that these two beliefs give me good reason to believe that q, jointly give me good reason to believe that q. And we are off on the infinite regress which Lewis Carroll made so famous.[2]

It will turn out, as I will argue below, that here too there is an empirical problem about a more modest version of this suggestion. The suggestion about reasoning follows the very pattern that we saw in the suggestion about knowledge and justification. Reflection is being called upon to solve a problem that it simply cannot solve.

Consider now the classic Frankfurt-style account of freedom of the will.[3] There is an important difference, Frankfurt insists, between young children and many non-human animals, on the one hand, and normal adult human beings, on the other. Young children and many animals have first-order beliefs and desires, Frankfurt allows, but they do not have second-order mental states. Human adults, however, not only have first-order mental states; they also have the benefit of having second-order states as well. Thus, consider a 3-year-old child who desires to have some candy and believes that there is candy available in the drawer. Other things being equal, the child will act on this belief–desire pair. The child's action will be jointly caused by her belief and desire, and the belief together with the desire will jointly rationalize the child's behavior. When the child acts in this way, according to Frankfurt, the child acts freely.

But adults are psychologically more complex. They not only have first-order beliefs and desires. They are capable of reflecting on those beliefs and desires, and, when they do so, they come to have beliefs about their first-order states, and they come to have preferences, or desires, for certain beliefs and desires. Thus, an adult may have a first-order desire to smoke a

---

[2] 'What the Tortoise Said to Achilles', *Mind*, 4 (1895), 278–80.
[3] 'Freedom of the Will and the Concept of a Person', repr. in *The Importance of What We Care about: Philosophical Essays* (Cambridge University Press, 1988), 11–25.

cigarette, and he may know where he can get ahold of some cigarettes. But the adult may also want to give up smoking, and, given the difficulty involved in doing so, may very much desire that he no longer have the desire to smoke. Someone else may not only have the first-order desire to smoke, but, on reflection, may fully endorse the idea of acting on that desire. Such a person comes to act not only on the basis of a first-order desire interacting with a first-order belief, as in the case of the young child, but on the basis of the interaction between the first-order states and what Frankfurt calls a second-order volition: a desire that a certain first-order desire—in this case, the desire to have a cigarette—be effective in producing action. It is only actions conforming to this more complex pattern involving second-order volitions, according to Frankfurt, that exemplify freedom of the will.

Having a free will, rather than merely acting freely, is extraordinarily important, according to Frankfurt. Creatures who lack second-order mental states, such as non-human animals and young children, cannot have a free will, and, according to Frankfurt, the fact that they have this very simple psychological structure robs them of personhood. It is a necessary condition of being a person, on Frankfurt's view, that one have second-order states, and that one engage in reflective self-evaluation. We will examine Frankfurt's view in detail, and others that have been influenced by it, in Chapter 3. Here, however, I would like to give a brief illustration of a way in which it falls into the same pattern as the views about knowledge, justification, and reasoning examined above.

Why is the status of personhood so important, and what are the advantages of having the more complicated psychological structure which having second-order mental states, and the ability to engage in critical reflection, allows? One part of the answer which Frankfurt gives is that someone who lacks second-order mental states is, in virtue of that very fact, 'a helpless bystander to the forces that move him'.[4] It is easy to see the worry here. An agent with first-order mental states, but no second-order states, and thus no ability to reflect upon them or to critically evaluate them, will inevitably be moved about by these first-order forces. And viewing such agents in this way seems to raise, in a rather direct way, a serious challenge to viewing them as agents at all. They do not act, it seems; they merely get pushed around by their psychological states.

---

[4] Ibid. 21.

But if this is one's worry about the status of individuals whose psychology involves nothing but first-order states, it should be clear that adding second-order psychological states can do nothing to alleviate the problem. If one is worried that the individual with a simple first-order psychology is pushed around by his internal states, it is no help at all to allow that there might be still more internal states, and more complicated ones, that do the pushing. Now maybe the initial worry about the relationship between an individual and that individual's psychological states is not a legitimate one. But we should agree that, if it is a legitimate worry, the appeal to second-order states, and to reflection, is not an adequate response.[5] The problem which arose at the first-order level arises just as much when we reflect and form second-order states.

Here too, I will argue that the problem is not a simple logical one. There are interesting empirical issues about what happens when we reflect upon our first-order states and critically evaluate our desires and the actions we might perform. We should not, I will argue, be enthusiastic about the value of such reflection across the board.

One last illustration. Some philosophers of a Kantian turn of mind have argued that the very content and force of normative demands—both the norms governing what we should believe and the norms governing how we should act—can only be understood by appreciating the crucial role which reflection plays in creating or constituting these demands. When we examine our first-order states, we find various beliefs and desires, and yet, as reflective creatures, we sometimes wonder whether we should believe or desire as we do, and whether we should act as we are, at times, tempted to act. How are we to answer such questions? What is the source of the normative demands which might provide answers to these questions? Christine Korsgaard offers the following suggestion:

If the problem springs from reflection then the solution must do so as well. If the problem is that our perceptions and desires might not withstand reflective scrutiny, then the solution is that they might. We need reasons because our impulses must be able to withstand reflective scrutiny. We have reasons if they do. The normative word 'reason' refers to a kind of reflective success.[6]

---

[5] This point echoes Gary Watson, 'Free Agency', *Journal of Philosophy*, 72 (1975), 205–20, esp. 218.

[6] *The Sources of Normativity* (Cambridge University Press, 1996), 93.

Here again, we see reflection being called upon to answer a problem that arises for our first-order states. And here, as elsewhere, I will argue that, once we understand the problem which arises at the first-order level, we will see that reflection could not possibly provide its solution. As with the other issues under discussion, I will argue that the problems that arise for reflection are not merely logical, but empirical as well. The psychology of human reflection is interesting, and interestingly different than we ordinarily take it to be.

Seeing these various problems side by side will, I hope, be revealing. There is a common structure to these issues, and by seeing it replayed in a number of different forums, we may come to better understand just what is at issue here and why it is that the appeal to reflection—however intuitive and commonsensical it may be—cannot do the work which it is so often called upon to perform. Once we have this in view, it should become clear that the picture of reflection which underlies all these attempts to recruit it as a philosophical problem solver is not only an unrealistic one. It is, instead, a picture which attributes magical powers to reflection, powers no psychological process could possibly have. This should serve to motivate a more realistic account of reflection, an account which demystifies it.[7]

I hope to provide at least the beginnings of such an account in the final chapter. Psychological research on the nature of reflection allows us to piece together a view of just what it is that reflection can and cannot do. This work is, of course, ongoing, and the conclusions reached here are inevitably tentative. But enough work has now been done, and there are enough robust results, to make the project of providing a realistic view of reflection one worth taking on.

---

[7] My project may thus be seen, in many ways, as the mirror-image of Keith Lehrer's project in his collection of papers, *Metamind* (Oxford University Press, 1990). Lehrer comments (pp. 1–2): 'These essays are also united by an underlying idea, one which became clearer to me over the years, and which motivated me to select these articles rather than others. The articles concern freedom, rational acceptance, social consensus, the analysis of knowledge, and, finally, Thomas Reid's philosophy of mind. What could possibly unify such a diverse collection of intellectual reflections?...The human mind is a metamind. Human freedom, rationality, consensus, knowledge, and conception depend on metamental operations and would not exist without such operations.' Like Lehrer, I see the topics of knowledge, rationality, reasoning, and freedom as related, but my claim here is that these do not essentially involve any sort of metamental operations.

1

Knowledge

Knowledge, it is widely held, requires justified, true belief. In order to be justified in holding a belief, however, it is often claimed that some sort of reflection on one's belief and its epistemic status is required. It is not hard to see why such a view is attractive. Consider a belief which is unreflectively arrived at. Suppose I am listening to a news report on the radio, and the newscaster states that the government's economic policies have resulted in an increase in unemployment. Suppose further that I simply believe what the newscaster says. I don't stop to think about whether this particular radio station, or this particular reporter, is a reliable source of information on economic issues. I don't stop to think about whether the station or the reporter have some sort of axe to grind on economic policy. And I don't stop to think about whether, given the other things I know about the government's policy and about unemployment, it is reasonable to claim that the government's current policy was responsible for the increase in unemployment. I'm busy making dinner, and I'm thinking about what to make for dinner, and when my wife is likely to get home, and whether I can get dinner on the table in a reasonable amount of time. The focus of my attention is not on economic issues, and I simply take on board what the newscaster says without giving it a second thought. In situations like this, it seems quite reasonable to say that the belief I form is not justified, and thus, that I fail to have knowledge, even if what the newscaster says is true, and even if the radio station and the newscaster are entirely reliable, and even if, given what I know about the government's policy and unemployment, it really is quite likely that government policy caused the current increase in unemployment. My failure to reflect on my belief and its epistemic status seems to show a defect in the way in which I arrived at my belief, a defect which makes my belief unjustified. A belief thus seems to be justified only if one has reflected upon its epistemic status.

In this chapter, we will examine views which make such critical reflection a necessary condition for knowledge, or, as certain authors do, for a special sort of knowledge.

1.1 The infinite regress

Consider the following example from Laurence BonJour, an example which has some of the same features as the example above.

Norman, under certain conditions which usually obtain, is a completely reliable clairvoyant with respect to certain kinds of subject matter. He possesses no evidence or reasons of any kind for or against the general possibility of such a cognitive power or for or against the thesis that he possesses it. One day Norman comes to believe that the President is in New York City, though he has no evidence either for or against this belief. In fact the belief is true and results from his clairvoyant power under circumstances in which it is completely reliable.[1]

BonJour argues that Norman is not justified in the belief which he forms, and he wishes to use this as an argument against a reliabilist account of justification. On such a view, an agent is justified in holding a belief just in case that belief is reliably produced, and since Norman's belief is reliably produced, reliabilists are committed to holding that Norman's belief in the circumstances described is actually justified. What is required for justification, according to reliabilists, is that some external relationship hold between an agent's belief and the world, not that the agent have a justified belief about such a relationship, or, indeed, that the agent have any sort of belief at all about the relationship between his belief and the world. BonJour argues that this is implausible, and, in particular, that it has implausible consequences in the case described:

Norman's acceptance of the belief about the President's whereabouts is epistemically irrational and irresponsible, and thereby unjustified, whether or not he believes himself to have clairvoyant power, so long as he has no justification for such a belief. Part of one's epistemic duty is to reflect critically on one's beliefs, and such critical reflection precludes believing things to which one has, to one's knowledge, no reliable means of epistemic access.[2]

---

[1] *The Structure of Empirical Knowledge* (Harvard University Press, 1985), 41.
[2] Ibid. 42.

There is then, according to BonJour, an epistemic duty to reflect critically upon one's beliefs, and Norman hasn't done that, just as in my example involving listening to the radio, I failed to reflect critically upon the claim that government policy is the source of an increase in the unemployment rate. When one fails to live up to one's epistemic duty, one has been epistemically irresponsible. But, according to BonJour, there is an essential connection between epistemic responsibility and justified belief.

My contention here is that the idea of avoiding such irresponsibility, of being epistemically responsible in one's believings, is the core of the notion of epistemic justification.[3]

So the problem with Norman's belief is not, as one might at first think, that he lacks evidence for it, although in the case described, Norman does in fact lack evidence for his belief. The problem here is that Norman has behaved as I did when listening to the radio: we both behaved in an epistemically irresponsible way because we formed a belief in a casual and unreflective manner. Norman was lucky, in that his belief was not only true, but reliably produced; but knowledge requires justification, and justification is not just a matter of getting lucky. It requires taking active steps to assure that one forms one's beliefs appropriately; and Norman hasn't done that.

Now if Norman had in fact bothered to reflect on the epistemic status of his belief, he would have noticed that he didn't have a shred of evidence for believing that he has clairvoyant powers, and, in the light of that, he didn't have a shred of evidence for believing that the President is in New York. But it is not this fact about what Norman would have noticed had he bothered to reflect which shows that he is unjustified. Rather, it is the simple fact that Norman didn't bother to engage in reflection which makes him unjustified. Reflection, on BonJour's view, is an epistemic duty. Failing to engage in reflection is epistemically irresponsible. If a belief is arrived at in a way which is epistemically irresponsible, it is not epistemically justified, and thus, fails to count as knowledge.

Thus, if we go back to the case in which I unreflectively form a belief about the effects of government economic policy simply on the basis of the newscaster's say-so, we see that it just doesn't matter, on BonJour's view,

---

[3] Ibid. 8.

whether I in fact have evidence that the radio station, and the reporter, are reliable, or whether the other beliefs I hold make it likely that what the newscaster said is true. None of this matters, on BonJour's view, because I failed to stop and reflect on the epistemic status of my belief,[4] and so the manner in which I formed my belief was irresponsible. Even if it would have turned out, had I bothered to stop and reflect, that I would have discovered that there is good reason to accept what the newscaster said, the fact remains that I didn't reflect, and so I didn't discover this, and so I am not justified, and I do not have knowledge. Without reflection, there is no justified belief; and without justified belief, there is no knowledge.

BonJour sets a high standard for justification and knowledge. Most of our beliefs are formed without the benefit of critical reflection, and so, on BonJour's view, most of our beliefs are not in fact justified, and we thus have precious little knowledge. But although BonJour is committed to the view that we have remarkably little knowledge, his view is not at all like traditional forms of skepticism. The traditional skeptic not only holds that, as a matter of fact, we have no knowledge. Rather, the skeptical claim is that knowledge is impossible. BonJour is not claiming anything like this at all. Indeed, quite the contrary. BonJour thinks that we are in a position to know a great deal, if only we would stop and reflect. It is our failure to reflect which robs us of knowledge, not some intrinsic impossibility of achieving it. The standard he sets may be high, but it is not an unreasonable standard, and it is well within our reach. Or so it seems.

---

[4] One might wonder whether I am being uncharitable to BonJour here. As I read BonJour, if Norman is to be justified, he must reflect on a certain higher-order question: the question of whether his belief that the President is in New York is justified. But one might think that what is necessary for justification is only that Norman reflect on a certain first-order question: Is the President really in New York? On this latter view, questions about Norman's beliefs as such need not be addressed. It is clear, however, that BonJour insists on the first and stronger of these two requirements. BonJour is at great pains to argue that 'the fact that a belief coherers [with one's other beliefs] is cognitively accessible to the believer himself, so that it can give *him* a reason for accepting the belief' (ibid. 101). Without such a requirement, as BonJour argues, his view simply becomes a version of externalism. More than this, BonJour makes clear that, in order to be justified in holding a belief, an agent must hold it in virtue of the recognition that it coheres with the agent's total body of beliefs, and this, in turn, requires that the agent have a grasp, or at least an approximate grasp, of his total system of beliefs (ibid. 101–6). This is an extraordinarily strong requirement, and it causes numerous problems for BonJour, leading, ultimately to his Doxastic Presumption. But all of these difficulties are caused by BonJour's recognition that anything less than this strong requirement would undermine his commitment to internalism. The consistent internalist is thus led, inevitably, to insist on the higher-order requirement.

We've seen that both Norman and I, in the examples described, have behaved in an epistemically irresponsible way because we have arrived at our beliefs without engaging in any sort of critical reflection. So let us examine what we would have had to do in order to arrive at our beliefs in a responsible way. Let us return to the kitchen, where I was listening to the radio while preparing dinner. Since it was my failure to reflect on the epistemic status of my belief which robbed me of justification, it seems that all I need to have done in order to gain justification would have been to stop and reflect on the epistemic status of my belief. So let us imagine a case in which I do that. I hear the newscaster say that government policies have caused a rise in the unemployment rate, and instead of uncritically believing what I hear, I stop to reflect. I'm tempted to believe what the newscaster says, I might think. But I ask myself whether I really have good reason to believe this.

Nothing, it seems, could be easier than meeting this demand. Thus, suppose that I believe that this particular radio station has been especially reliable in its reporting on economic issues, and that the particular reporter involved is one of the radio station's most reliable reporters. If I note, on reflection, that I have these beliefs, then this is certainly a good start. But, of course, merely believing these things is not sufficient for justification. So I need to reflect on the epistemic status of these beliefs to see whether they are justified. A familiar regress argument here seems to force a choice among foundationalism, coherentism, and infinitism, and there are familiar difficulties with each of these views.[5] But let us not worry about these issues, and let us assume that some satisfactory resolution can be found to this choice. There is, nevertheless, another regress lurking, and it is one that has to do with reflection itself.

When I reflect on the claim that the government's policies are the source of rising unemployment, I form beliefs about my own beliefs—for example, that I believe the radio station to be reliable—and I form beliefs about the extent to which these beliefs provide epistemic reason for thinking that the government's policies are the source of rising unemployment. One might think that reflection provides me with excellent access to the contents of my beliefs; we are, one might think,

---

[5] These choices are presented in a particularly clear way in William Alston, 'Two Types of Foundationalism', *Journal of Philosophy*, 73 (1976), 165–85.

extremely reliable about what it is that we believe.[6] But there is also the problem of assessing the extent to which these beliefs provide epistemic support for the belief about the unemployment rate, and this is, to be sure, a complicated question. I might be very good at assessing this sort of thing, or I might not. The important point here, however, is that, in making these various judgments about my first-order beliefs and their epistemic relationship to the target belief, it is not my reliability itself which is at issue. Norman, after all, was assumed to be perfectly reliable in forming judgments like the one he made about the President. Whatever one's reliability in making a judgment, BonJour's view is that the judgment itself is epistemically irresponsible unless it has been subjected to reflective scrutiny. So even if I am perfectly reliable in figuring out what my beliefs are, and even if I am perfectly reliable in figuring out the extent to which they support the target belief, this entire edifice of belief is irresponsibly arrived at, and therefore unjustified, if it contains beliefs which have not been subjected to reflective scrutiny. But now we see that reflecting on one's first-order beliefs—and thereby forming (second-order) beliefs about them—is not enough, for this only creates the need for subjecting these second-order beliefs to reflective scrutiny. And reflecting on these beliefs (and thereby forming third-order beliefs about them) would not be enough either, for this would only create the need for still higher-order beliefs; and so on. An infinite regress results. No amount of reflective scrutiny is ever enough, for, wherever one stops reflecting, there is always some belief playing a would-be justificatory role which has itself gone unreflected upon. On the view BonJour articulates, this assures the impossibility of forming justified beliefs, and therefore, the impossibility of having knowledge.

---

[6] This supposition, I believe, vastly oversimplifies what is at issue here. Suppose e.g. that one holds a coherence theory of justification, as BonJour, in fact, does (in the book under discussion). In that case, whatever claim one wishes to evaluate, all of one's beliefs are relevant in assessing its justificatory status. But then one must begin the process of assessment by determining exactly what the content is of one's entire corpus of beliefs. Such a task is not just difficult; it is something which no human agent is capable of. BonJour is quite frank about the difficulties this presents for his view. (See *Structure of Empirical Knowledge*, 101–2.) I have discussed these difficulties in detail in 'The Unattainability of Coherence', in Bender (1989: 207–14). But even if one is not a coherence theorist, the task of identifying all of one's relevant beliefs—think here especially of complicated cases involving inference to an explanation—is highly non-trivial.

Thus, contrary to initial impressions, this requirement that we engage in reflective assessment of our beliefs is not easily satisfied; indeed, it is not satisfiable. Any view which makes this a requirement for justified belief, or knowledge, leads to total skepticism.

1.2 Two kinds of knowledge?

One way to avoid this problem is to draw a distinction between two different kinds of knowledge, one of which requires reflection, and one of which does not. Of course, the kind of knowledge which requires reflection must be defined in a way which avoids the infinite regress, but it is possible to do this by drawing on the idea that there is also another sort of knowledge which is less demanding. Thus, Ernest Sosa draws a distinction between what he calls *animal knowledge* and *reflective knowledge*:

> One has *animal knowledge* about one's environment, one's past, and one's own experience if one's judgments and beliefs about these are direct responses to their impact—e.g., through perception or memory—with little or no benefit of reflection or understanding.
> One has *reflective knowledge* if one's judgment or belief manifests not only such direct response to the fact known but also understanding of its place in a wider whole that includes one's belief and knowledge of it and how these come about.[7]

What Sosa attempts to do here is resolve the debate between internalists and externalists in an amicable way. If Sosa is right, there are really two different sorts of knowledge, one of which—animal knowledge—is very much the sort that externalists have long defended. It requires, roughly, reliably produced belief. As long as one's true belief stands in the right sort of relationship to the external world—regardless of whether one has any beliefs about that relationship—the belief counts as knowledge, at least in this weaker sense. The second sort of knowledge—reflective knowledge—attempts to capture a good deal of what internalists have been after, for reflective knowledge requires some appreciation of the relationship between one's target belief, and one's other beliefs, and the external world. Instead of seeing internalism and externalism as rivals, Sosa attempts

---

[7] 'Knowledge and Intellectual Virtue', repr. in *Knowledge in Perspective: Selected Essays in Epistemology* (Cambridge University Press, 1991), 225–44; the quotation is from p. 240. A similar characterization is found in Sosa's 'Reflective Knowledge in the Best Circles', *Journal of Philosophy*, 94 (1997), 410–30.

to provide a view on which they are complementary. Each is (roughly) right about one sort of knowledge.[8]

This way of presenting things allows Sosa to escape the infinite regress presented in section 1.1. Reflective knowledge requires that one's first-order judgment be subjected to reflective scrutiny, and the resulting reflective judgments about the first-order target belief must themselves meet some non-trivial epistemic standards. After all, it would hardly make sense to suggest that there is some sort of high-grade knowledge that we may achieve if only we reflect on our first-order beliefs, and then allow that the reflective judgments on these beliefs may be completely inaccurate or unreliable. It would be difficult to see why reflection of this sort would add to the quality of one's knowledge. Sosa thus requires that the second-order beliefs which reflection produces manifest some sort of *understanding* of how the first-order belief came about, as well as an understanding of its relationship to one's other beliefs. I take it that understanding here requires some sort of knowledge. To insist that it requires reflective knowledge would generate the infinite regress. The regress is avoided, however, if the knowledge that reflection produces need not itself be reflective. When we reflect on our (first-order) belief, and its relationship to our other beliefs, and how it came about, we need only achieve animal knowledge about these matters. Reflective knowledge thus understood avoids the infinite regress.

We thus have a well-defined distinction here and, more than that, by defining reflective knowledge in a way that avoids the regress, we have two kinds of knowledge each of which seems well within our reach. Not

---

[8] This is so, at least, in 'Knowledge and Intellectual Virtue' and in 'Reflective Knowledge in the Best Circles'. In more recent work, Sosa's account of the distinction between reflective knowledge and animal knowledge has changed. Thus, in *A Virtue Epistemology: Apt Belief and Reflective Knowledge*, i (Oxford University Press, 2007), Sosa now defines animal knowledge as apt belief (roughly, reliably produced true belief), and reflective knowledge as 'apt belief aptly noted', i.e. true belief which is both reliably produced and also such that one has a reliably produced true belief that the first-order belief was reliably produced (ibid. 34, 43, 98, 113). But this new definition of reflective knowledge is just animal knowledge twice over. It requires no knowledge (reflective or otherwise) of how one's first-order belief came about or its relationship to one's other beliefs. And this severs the connection, I would argue, between reflective knowledge so defined and internalist motivations and intuitions. I should point out, however, that Sosa disagrees with this characterization of his view. In response to this complaint, Sosa remarks, 'My new emphasis on the KK principle, on reflective knowledge as apt belief aptly noted, is just a streamlining of the same former view.' 'Replies to Commentators on *A Virtue Epistemology*', *Philosophical Studies*, 144 (2009), 144.

every well-defined distinction, however, is worth making. We could define two different sorts of knowledge, one sort acquired on even-numbered days of the month, and the other acquired on odd-numbered days, but there would be little point in making such a distinction. We need to know why the distinction between animal knowledge and reflective knowledge is an illuminating one. Sosa has a good deal to say about this.

Let us therefore consider two individuals, Jack and Jill, each of whom know that p. Jack has animal knowledge that p, but he lacks reflective knowledge; Jill, however, has reflective knowledge that p. Thus, let us suppose that Jack has a reliably produced true belief that p, but he has not reflected on the fact that he has this belief, nor has he thought about its source, or its relationship to his other beliefs. Jill, on the other hand, not only has a reliably produced true belief that p, but she has thought about these issues, and, as a result of reflection, she has reliably produced true beliefs about how she came to believe that p, about the relationship between p and her other beliefs, and about the reliability of the process by which she came to believe that p. Is Jill's knowledge that p superior in any way to Jack's?

Jill, of course, knows a great deal that Jack does not. Jack does not know about his other beliefs; he therefore does not know about the relationship between his belief that p and his other beliefs; and he has no knowledge of the process by which his belief that p was produced, nor does he know whether that process, whatever it may be, is reliable. Jill knows all of these things. But our question was not whether Jill knows things that Jack does not. Clearly, she does. The question was whether Jill's knowledge that p is in any way superior to Jack's. If knowing these other things makes Jill's knowledge that p better than Jack's, we need to know how it does so.

Perhaps the most natural thought here is that, because Jill has subjected her belief to extra scrutiny, her belief that p is not only reliably produced, but it is more reliably produced than Jack's belief. The whole point in subjecting one's beliefs to reflective scrutiny, it might seem, is to increase one's reliability. Sosa suggests something very much like this. The benefit of the additional knowledge Jill has—her understanding of the source and reliability of her belief that p—may be explained in these very terms.

Since a direct response supplemented by such understanding would in general have a better chance of being right, reflective knowledge is better justified than corresponding animal knowledge.[9]

But it is not at all clear that this is correct.

First, Jill need not be more reliable than Jack. Jack's first-order process of belief acquisition may be extremely reliable. The fact that Jill has arrived at the same belief as Jack, and subjected it to additional scrutiny, tells us nothing about whether she is more reliable, even after this additional scrutiny, than Jack is.

Now one might think that this misses the point. The real question we should be asking is not whether Jill is more reliable than Jack. After all, if Jill's first-order process of belief acquisition were quite different from Jack's, and, in particular, if it were far less reliable, then it would be no surprise should Jill's belief that p be less reliably produced than Jack's belief. The comparison we should be interested in is between Jill's belief that p before she reflected—when she had mere animal knowledge that p—and Jill's belief that p after reflection, once she had attained reflective knowledge. Is there reason to believe, as Sosa suggests, that by subjecting one's first-order belief to reflective scrutiny, we thereby make it more likely that it be true, on the assumption, of course, that it passes reflective muster?

The suggestion that subjecting our beliefs to reflective scrutiny makes them more likely to be true is extremely attractive. Our motivation in scrutinizing our beliefs, of course, is precisely to provide an extra check on them. It is thus quite natural to believe that when they survive this scrutiny, they are more likely to be true than beliefs which have gone unchecked. But the question about the value of reflective monitoring is not a trivial one. Just as first-order beliefs which have gone unscrutinized may be reliably produced or, alternatively, the product of unreliable processes, the processes by which we reflectively check on first-order beliefs may themselves be reliable, or instead, quite unreliable. The mere fact that we have applied some additional check on our first-order beliefs tells us nothing about the reliability of the checking procedure. Moreover, if the first-order process of belief acquisition was itself sufficiently reliable to begin with, then reflective scrutiny of the process is completely

---

[9] 'Knowledge and Intellectual Virtue', 240.

unnecessary. Nothing is gained by checking up on a process which is virtually assured of producing a true belief in any case. Finally, these two points about the value of reflective checking interact with one another. If the first-order process of belief acquisition is especially reliable, and the reflective process of checking is far less reliable, the value of reflective scrutiny is especially low. This is so even if the reflective process is reliable enough to produce knowledge. The question of whether reflective knowledge that p is superior to animal knowledge that p thus comes down to a question about the reliability of reflective scrutiny. But to say this, I believe, is to challenge the significance of the distinction between animal and reflective knowledge.

Consider an analogy. Suppose that I have a handful of friends whom I trust a great deal, and I frequently consult with them before reaching a conclusion about matters of importance. When an issue arises that matters to me, I think things through, and then consult with my friends. I not only ask them what I should believe about the relevant matter, I also ask them for their reasons, and what it is that they know about related issues.[10] Let us leave aside, for a moment, the issue of my friends' reliability, and whether the beliefs I come to as a result of these consultations are more or less likely to be true than beliefs arrived at independently of these friends; let us also leave aside the reasons, if any, I have for trusting them. One of the results of my consultations is that I come to have a wider range of beliefs than I would have had without consulting. On occasions on which I consult with my friends, I thus have a larger and more deeply interconnected[11] body of beliefs than I otherwise would. I also come to have greater confidence in the beliefs I reach after consulting my friends than the ones I arrive at without consultation.

Let us call the knowledge I come to have after consulting with my friends *consultative knowledge*, and knowledge which I have which is not screened by these friends *non-consultative knowledge*. Suppose I come to believe that consultative knowledge is superior to non-consultative knowledge. Indeed, I recognize that, while other people do form their

[10] The analogy with reflection will be even closer if we suppose that the friends I consult show a certain deference to my opinions, tending to encourage me to believe just what I would have believed even without consultation, as we will see in section 1.3 below.

[11] Sosa emphasizes the fact that reflection produces a body of beliefs which are connected in this way. See *A Virtue Epistemology*, 113, and *Reflective Knowledge: Apt Belief and Reflective Knowledge*, ii (Oxford University Press, 2009), 143, 189–94.

beliefs in ways which benefit from the testimony of others, very few if any others have a group of friends on whom they rely in just the way I do to inform my epistemic decisions. And suppose that I come to believe, as a result, that the knowledge which others have, since it is merely non-consultative, is inferior to mine.

Would I be justified in drawing a distinction between these two alleged kinds of knowledge, and would I be correct in thinking that consultative knowledge is superior to non-consultative knowledge? As far as the first question goes, it seems to me that so-called consultative knowledge is not a different kind of knowledge from non-consultative knowledge. Yes, in order to possess consultative knowledge, one must have gone through a certain process which the possessor of non-consultative knowledge has not followed. But if this is a ground for drawing a distinction between different kinds of knowledge, then we will have as many different kinds of knowledge as there are processes of belief acquisition and retention. Surely this multiplies kinds of knowledge far beyond necessity. On the second question, it seems that until we know something about the reliability of my friends, the question of whether going through the additional consultation improves my epistemic situation remains unanswered. If my friends are like most, and they are reliable about some areas and unreliable about others, then the epistemic value of my checking with them will be a mixed bag. But, to return to my first point, even in the unlikely event that this checking increases my reliability across the board, it hardly seems right to suggest that consultative knowledge is a different sort of knowledge than that possessed by others. We may better address the epistemic issues involved here by asking about the advantages and disadvantages of consultation with a small circle of friends than by introducing a distinction between different sorts of knowledge.

It seems to me that the distinction between reflective knowledge and animal knowledge is no better grounded than the distinction between consultative and non-consultative knowledge. There is no ground, I believe, for regarding reflective knowledge and animal knowledge as two different sorts of knowledge, nor is there adequate ground for thinking that knowledge which is produced or sustained by means of reflection is, eo ipso, better knowledge than knowledge which does not draw upon reflection. The epistemic utility of reflection is, to my mind, an interesting and important topic, but it is most clearly addressed directly. Insisting on a distinction between animal knowledge and reflective knowledge gets in the way of, rather than aids, such an assessment.

Let us turn, then, to an examination of the processes involved in reflection, and their effects on the reliability of the processes by which our beliefs are produced and sustained.

1.3 Does reflective scrutiny improve our reliability?[12]

Often, we form beliefs unreflectively. This, when things are working as they should, produces what Sosa calls *animal knowledge*. But sometimes we stop and reflect on the beliefs which we have unreflectively formed, or we stop and reflect on beliefs we are tempted to form. We scrutinize these beliefs or potential beliefs, and if they pass scrutiny, we either continue to hold the belief or, in the case where we were only tempted to hold the belief, we adopt the belief for the first time. As Sosa remarks in the passage quoted above, what reflective knowledge adds to mere animal knowledge is 'understanding of [the first-order belief's] place in a wider whole that includes one's belief and knowledge of it and how these come about'. So when we reflect, we often consider the source of our first-order belief— how it came about—as well as its relationship to our other beliefs. We think about whether we have good reason to hold the belief in question. But what actually happens when we engage in this kind of reflection? To what extent are we able to accurately identify the source of our beliefs in order to aid us in the task of deciding whether we should go on holding them? And to what extent are we able to figure out our evidential situation? Just how reliable are we at identifying the other beliefs we hold which are relevant to evaluating the target belief? And when we do identify these other beliefs, how well do we perform the evaluation itself? We need to address all of these questions if we are to have any idea of the effectiveness of engaging in reflective scrutiny.

When we stop to reflect on the source of our beliefs, we do often come to form (second-order) beliefs about the source of our first-order

---

[12] Here I summarize and extend results which I first presented in 'Introspection and Misdirection', *Australasian Journal of Philosophy*, 67 (1989), 410–22, and which I developed in *Knowledge and its Place in Nature* (Oxford University Press, 2002), ch. 4.

judgments. If you ask people why they hold the beliefs they do, then, in a very wide variety of cases, they will give quite confident answers about how they arrived at their beliefs. It is, however, well-known that a very large part of the cognitive processes by which beliefs are produced is unavailable to introspection. For example, the vast majority of the information processing that goes on in visual perception simply eludes introspection; one can't even begin to understand the complexity of the psychological processes involved in vision by introspective means.[13] The same is true, of course, of the processes involved in language acquisition and use.[14] Indeed, this is true of belief acquisition generally. The parts of these processes that even seem to be available to introspection are just the tip of the iceberg. One can't do cognitive psychology by simply reflecting on one's mental processes.

All of this is to say that the view we have of the processes by which our beliefs are produced, when we reflect on our beliefs, is at best partial. But this might not be a problem if the part of the process which we seem to have access to allows us to accurately evaluate the reliability of the entire process. Thus, for example, if any errors we might be making are most likely to show up, or leave some trace, in the parts of the process which are available to introspection, then reflective evaluation of the source of our beliefs might be an extremely useful thing. So we need to know to what extent the view we have of belief acquisition, when we reflect, can contribute to an accurate evaluation of the reliability of that process. And since the point of reflective evaluation of these processes is amelioration, we will be especially interested in whether errors we might otherwise make, were we unreflective, are likely to be identified when we stop to reflect.

The beliefs we form are often influenced in powerful ways by factors which do not in any way make it likely that the resulting beliefs are true. Our beliefs about the quality of various consumer goods may be influenced by their relative position: we have a strong tendency to believe that objects further to the right are superior to objects further to the left.[15] We

[13] For one particularly useful account of these processes, see David Marr, *Vision* (W. H. Freeman, 1982).

[14] For an early and important account, see Noam Chomsky, *Aspects of the Theory of Syntax* (MIT Press, 1965).

[15] Richard Nisbett and Timothy Wilson, 'Telling More than we Can Know: Verbal Reports on Mental Processes', *Psychological Review*, 84 (1977), 231–59. At least this is one possible source of the phenomenon Nisbett and Wilson discuss. It may be instead that the bias is

are influenced in the numerical judgments we make when, in the course of arriving at our judgments, we are exposed to obviously irrelevant numerical information. Thus, for example, subjects who were asked to estimate how many African countries are members of the United Nations were dramatically influenced in their judgments by the number which turned up on the spin of a roulette wheel.[16] We are influenced in our interactions with others, and the beliefs we form about them, by simple exposure to words such as 'rude' or 'polite'.[17] The colors of objects influence our judgments about a variety of matters in ways which are completely unreliable.[18] We are influenced by stimuli presented below the threshold of awareness, and these influences are often only randomly correlated, or negatively correlated, with the truth of the resulting beliefs.[19] Our judgments are often influenced by racial stereotypes, even when we do not believe the very features of those stereotypes which play a crucial role in affecting our judgments.[20] In all of these cases, subjects are unaware that their beliefs are influenced by these extraneous factors. When directly asked whether their judgments are influenced in these ways, subjects deny, often quite vehemently, that their beliefs were

not spatial, but temporal (since the objects on the right were examined after the ones on the left). On this point, see also Wilson and Nisbett, 'The Accuracy of Verbal Reports about the Effects of Stimuli on Evaluations and Behavior', *Social Psychology*, 41 (1978), 118–31. It is quite clear not only that reflection is powerless to detect the source of these judgments, but that the experimental investigation of this issue is no trivial matter either. I am indebted to an anonymous referee for this point.

[16] Amos Tversky and Daniel Kahneman, 'Judgment under Uncertainty: Heuristics and Biases', *Science*, 185 (1974), 1124–31.

[17] J. A. Bargh, M. Chen, and L. Burrows, 'Automaticity of Social Behavior: Direct Effects of Trait Construct and Stereotype Activation on Action', *Journal of Personality and Social Psychology*, 71 (1996), 230–44.

[18] Thus e.g. judgments about politicians were found to be influenced by the colors of their campaign posters (in ways having nothing to do e.g. with the ways in which certain colors may reliably indicate the party of which the politician is a member) in Rubinoff and March, 'Candidates and Color: An Investigation', *Perceptual and Motor Skills*, 50 (1980), 868–70. The color of ballots was found to influence voting behavior in Garret and Brooks, 'Effect of Ballot Color, Sex of Candidate, and Sex of College Students of Voting Age on their Voting Behavior', *Psychological Reports*, 60 (1987), 39–44. The importance of color of packaging has long been known to those in advertising and sales, and often used to great advantage. See e.g. Fehrman and Fehrman, *Color: The Secret Influence*, 2nd edn. (Prentice-Hall, 2003).

[19] P. M. Merikle, 'Perception without Awareness: Critical Issues', *American Psychologist*, 47 (1992), 792–5.

[20] P. G. Devine, 'Stereotypes and Prejudice: Their Automatic and Controlled Components', *Journal of Personality and Social Psychology*, 56 (1989), 5–18. And see Marc Hauser's Moral Sense Test, at http://moral.wjh.harvard.edu/index2.html

affected in any way by the factors which played the most direct causal role in bringing about their beliefs.[21] Ziva Kunda nicely summarizes the upshot of this large body of literature.

Our judgments, feelings, and behaviors can be influenced by factors that we have never been aware of and have only been exposed to subliminally, by factors that we were aware of at one time but can no longer recall, and by factors that we can still recall but whose influence we are unaware of.[22]

Asking subjects to introspect more carefully, or think longer and harder about the sources of their beliefs, is entirely useless in many of these cases.[23] Subjects are often ignorant of the actual source of their beliefs, and reflection is, in many cases, incapable of revealing it to them.

This does not mean, however, that when subjects in these cases reflect on the source of their beliefs, they find themselves at a loss or recognize that they are ignorant on the issue of how their beliefs came about. Nothing like this is true. Instead, subjects in these examples offer quite confident accounts of the source of their beliefs, accounts which are not even close to correct. By and large, the accounts they offer serve to rationalize their beliefs. Were these accounts correct, they would serve to show how it is that the subjects arrived at their beliefs on the basis of good reasons.[24] Finally, the phenomenology of these subjects is quite interesting. These subjects do not seem to themselves to be offering

---

[21] See Nisbett and Wilson, 'Telling More than we Can Know'.

[22] Ziva Kunda, *Social Cognition: Making Sense of People* (MIT Press, 1999), 308.

[23] Laurence BonJour, in an attempt to defend reflection against the kind of concerns developed here, suggests otherwise, although he offers no experimental evidence for his claim. I have not been able to find any experimental evidence at all which suggests that BonJour is right here. See BonJour, 'Kornblith on Knowledge and Epistemology', *Philosophical Studies*, 127 (2006), esp. 324–6. Richard Feldman also suggests, in a case of this sort, that one might be able to discover the source of one's belief by way of reflection, but he too offers no experimental evidence. See Feldman, 'Chisholm's Internalism and its Consequences', *Metaphilosophy*, 34 (2003), 607. It is not my view that reflection can never help. Such a view would be no more reasonable than the view that it always does. Here, as elsewhere, the question at issue is a difficult empirical one, and one should not form a judgment on this issue merely on the basis of one's belief that one has, at times, engaged in reflection on issues of this sort and resolved them satisfactorily. One's impression that one has successfully resolved such issues requires experimental confirmation. Nicholas Epley and Thomas Gilovich have a nice discussion of some cases where reflective engagement does and does not make a difference. See their 'When Effortful Thinking Influences Judgmental Anchoring: Differential Effects of Forewarning and Incentives on Self-Generated and Externally Provided Anchors', *Journal of Behavioral Decision Making*, 18 (2005), 199–212.

[24] Nisbett and Wilson, 'Telling More than We Can Know'.

some sort of retrospective hypothesis about how it is that they must have arrived at their beliefs. Rather, it seems to them that they are directly aware of the manner in which they arrived at their beliefs. Their self-knowledge, as they see it, is as direct as self-knowledge ever is.[25]

Thus, in an extremely wide variety of cases, subjects form beliefs in ways which are quite unreliable. They are moved by factors of which they are unaware, and reflection on the source of their beliefs cannot make them aware of these factors. When they do stop to reflect, however, they come to form confident beliefs about how it is that they arrived at their first-order beliefs. These judgments, which are entirely inaccurate, portray them as properly moved by good reasons. These judgments about the source of their first-order beliefs seem to be direct and unmediated by inference or theorizing. What these subjects are doing, however, is confabulating.[26] These subjects are sincere in their claims about the sources of their beliefs, and they are entirely taken in by their own confabulation. Moreover, these subjects are not all facing situations which are contrived or unrealistic. The factors which influence them are regularly present in our everyday environment. We are all subject to these influences, and we are all bound to form an immense number of beliefs in these unreliable ways, despite the fact that, when we reflect on these very beliefs, we each seem to ourselves to be a paradigm of rationality.

The idea, then, that by reflecting on the source of our beliefs, we may thereby subject them to some sort of proper screening, and thereby improve on the accuracy of the resulting beliefs, is simply misguided. When we reflect in this way, we get the impression that we are actually providing some sort of extra screening of our beliefs, and we thus have the very strong impression that we are actually doing something to assure that

---

[25] Alison Gopnik, 'How We Know our Minds: The Illusion of First-Person Knowledge of Intentionality', *Behavioral and Brain Sciences*, 16 (1993), 1–15 and 90–101; Nisbett and Wilson, 'Telling More than We Can Know'.

[26] Peter Wason and Jonathan St. B. T. Evans, 'Dual Processing in Reasoning', *Cognition*, 3 (1975), 141–54; Nisbett and Wilson, 'Telling More than We Can Know'; Timothy Wilson, *Strangers to Ourselves: Discovering the Adaptive Unconscious* (Harvard University Press, 2002); E. J. Lucas and L. J. Ball, 'Think-Aloud Protocols and the Selection Task: Evidence for Relevance Effects and Rationalisation Processes', *Thinking and Reasoning*, 11 (2005), 35–66. Jamin Halberstadt and Timothy Wilson, 'Reflections on Conscious Reflection: Mechanisms of Impairment by Reasons Analysis', in Adler and Rips (2008: 548–65); Marc Hauser *et al.*, 'A Dissociation between Moral Judgments and Justifications', *Mind and Language*, 22 (2007), 1–21. For a nice discussion of confabulation, see Peter Carruthers, *The Opacity of Mind: An Integrative Theory of Self-Knowledge* (Oxford University Press, 2011), 339–45.

our beliefs are, indeed, reliably arrived at. But this is not what we are doing at all. Instead, we are engaged in a process which, in a very wide range of cases, makes us more confident that we are right than before we began, but a process, nevertheless, which is almost useless for improving our reliability. In a large class of cases, the process of reflection is an exercise in self-congratulation. It does nothing, however, in these important cases, to improve on the accuracy of our first-order beliefs.

We have a number of general tendencies which aid in this process of self-misunderstanding. We have a very strong tendency to persevere in the beliefs we form. Once we do form a belief, we are strongly disposed to scrutinize evidence against it, and we are usually able to come up with commonsensical explanations for why the evidence should not be trusted in this particular case. Evidence in favor of beliefs we already hold, however, is not so carefully scrutinized, and it is typically taken at face value. In addition, our memory is not even-handed in the way it treats evidence for and against the beliefs we hold. Evidence in favor of existing beliefs is better remembered than evidence against them. When we do stop to reflect on our beliefs and scrutinize the evidence we can remember, it is no surprise that we find our beliefs to be well-supported by the available evidence. The ways in which memory and reflection work strongly bias the results of our self-examination in ways conducive to that result.[27] It should come as no surprise, then, that there is a large psychological literature on overconfidence, showing that, for an important range of judgments, we tend to believe that we are far more accurate than, in fact, we are.[28] Far from providing the solution to this particular problem, reflection is itself an important source of the problem.[29]

---

[27] Richard Nisbett and Lee Ross, *Human Inference: Strategies and Shortcomings of Social Judgment* (Prentice-Hall, 1980), ch. 8.

[28] See e.g. Alan Garnham and Jane Oakhill, *Thinking and Reasoning* (Blackwell, 1994), 158–60; Ziva Kunda, *Social Cognition: Making Sense of People*, 65–7; Keith Stanovich, *Who is Rational? Studies of Individual Differences in Reasoning* (Laurence Erlbaum, 1999), 116–21; as well as papers in Kahneman *et al.* (eds), *Judgment under Uncertainty: Heuristics and Biases* (Cambridge University Press, 1982), part VI; and papers in Gilovich *et al.* (eds), *Heuristics and Biases: The Psychology of Intuitive Judgment* (Cambridge University Press, 2002), part I, sections C and D.

[29] Thus, although Sherrilyn Roush rightly emphasizes the benefits that recalibration can bring ('Second Guessing: A Self-Help Manual', *Episteme*, forthcoming), it would be a mistake to think that such recalibration can best be accomplished under the guidance of mere reflection.

I have focused here on cases where our first-order beliefs are both mistaken and unreliably produced because these are the cases in which the need for amelioration is most urgent, and where the act of reflecting on our beliefs might seem best suited for providing some sort of epistemic improvement. Given the way in which reflection works in these cases, there seems little reason to agree with Sosa that reflective knowledge is superior to mere animal knowledge in virtue of the additional reliability which reflection provides. Reflection, by and large, does not provide for greater reliability. It does not, by and large, serve to guard against errors to which we would otherwise be susceptible. It does not, by and large, aid in the much needed project of cognitive self-improvement. It creates the illusion that it does all of these things, but it does not do any of them.

1.4 Are there other benefits that reflection provides?

Sosa does not rest his case for the superiority of reflective knowledge over animal knowledge on the claim of reliability alone. He makes several other claims about its value as well.[30] First, according to Sosa, reflection plays a unique and foundational role in self-assessment. Other potential sources of belief or change of belief can only be properly assessed, Sosa suggests, by way of reflection.[31] Second, Sosa argues that only reflection can explain the traditional importance of skepticism.[32] And finally, third, there is an important connection, Sosa suggests, between reflection and epistemic agency.[33] We will need to examine each of these claims.

So let us consider the first of Sosa's three claims, that reflection plays a special role in self-assessment. There is no doubt that we engage, at times, in self-assessment by way of reflection, but there are many different mental processes and sources of information which we may draw on when we engage in self-assessment. Thus, as I pointed out earlier, we may consult

---

[30] Indeed, in *A Virtue Epistemology: Apt Belief and Reflective Knowledge*, i, Sosa no longer claims that reflective knowledge provides for greater reliability than animal knowledge. The importance and advantages of reflective knowledge are located elsewhere.

[31] See 'Replies', in John Greco (ed.), *Ernest Sosa and his Critics* (Blackwell, 2004), 291. BonJour suggests something quite similar in his 'Kornblith on Knowledge and Epistemology', 329–33.

[32] Ibid. 292.

[33] Ibid.

with others in order to check on the accuracy of our beliefs. Why should we think that reflective knowledge is superior to animal knowledge in a way that consultative knowledge is not? Here is what Sosa says.

No matter how much we value consultation, we are unwilling to yield our intellectual autonomy, which requires us to assess the place of consultation in the light of all our other relevant information and recognized desiderata. For, to assess it thus is to evaluate it in the light of reflection. Of course, reflection itself might benefit from consultative evaluation. So, why put reflection above consultation? Partly, it seems to me, because the deliverances of consultation need assessing in the light of reflection in a way that is different from how reflection is to be assessed through consultation. In the end, reflection has properly a closer, more fully determinative influence on the beliefs we form, and the deliverances of consultation bear properly only through reflection's sifting and balancing.[34]

We will need to unpack this a bit.

When we assess the value, for example, of consulting with others, we may do so by way of reflection. We focus on the beliefs we form when we consult, and we consider, for example, the extent to which such a process improves our reliability. More than this, what is true of consultation seems to be true of other means of arriving at our beliefs. To the extent that we are interested in evaluating them, we may bring reflection to bear on that task. Reflection thus seems to hold a privileged place among the many different cognitive processes we may bring to bear in forming and revising our beliefs. It seems to play an ineliminable foundational role.

Now Sosa is aware that reflection itself can be evaluated, and that when we evaluate it, we bring other processes to bear on that evaluation. Thus, as he points out, we may evaluate the virtues of reflection by, among other things, consulting with others. Alternatively, we may engage in experimental research to determine the reliability of reflection. But even when we do this, Sosa suggests, reflection continues to play an ineliminable role. These other processes which we draw on in evaluating reflection 'bear properly only through reflection's sifting and balancing'. And this serves, on Sosa's view, to differentiate reflection from other processes. It plays a unique and ineliminable role in any self-evaluation.

I don't believe, however, that Sosa is correct about this. Consider, for example, any of the experimental psychologists who are interested in the question of the reliability of reflection. They could, for example, simply

---

[34] Ibid. 291.

reflect on this question instead of performing experiments and, no doubt, if they did so they would find that, when they reflect, it certainly seems as if reflection is quite reliable. But, of course, this is not what they do. Instead, they perform experiments which aim to test whether reflection genuinely is reliable. Now Sosa seems to suggest that, even if they do this, reflection will inevitably play a role in this evaluation. It is hard to see, however, why it must. The psychologists produce a good bit of data in performing their experiments and, no doubt, they think at some length about the data and what would best explain the data. People sometimes use the word 'reflec-tion' in quite a broad sense to refer to any act of thinking, and so they will speak of these experimenters as reflecting on the data and their proper explanation. But this has nothing to do with the kind of reflection which is under discussion here. The process of reflection under discussion involves thinking about one's own first-order mental states in a first-personal way. So someone who 'reflects' on a body of data is not reflecting in our sense, nor is someone who theorizes in a third-person manner about how his or her own mental states are influenced by various factors. So the experimentalist who attempts to evaluate reflection in our sense (and this is the sense in which I will continue to use the term throughout this book), or who attempts to evaluate any other psychological process, need not make use of reflection at all in performing the evaluation. Indeed, experimental psychologists who are familiar with the literature cited in section 1.3 are extremely unlikely to make use of reflection in their evaluation since they are likely to believe that such a process of evaluation would be unreliable. Thinking about one's own mental processes from a first-person point of view is not a necessary part of any evaluation.

Now one might try to defend the claim that reflection is necessary for a proper evaluation of any psychological process in a slightly different way. Thus, for example, Laurence BonJour discusses the kinds of experimental study surveyed above and raises some questions about them.

I want to ask two related questions about such studies. First, do the investigators in question have any good *reasons*, reasons that they can be reflectively aware of and could in principle cite to others, for believing that the alleged results of the study are in fact probably correct? Second, do those same investigators have any good *reasons* for believing that the methods that were employed in the studies are in fact reliable?[35]

---

[35] 'Kornblith on Knowledge and Epistemology', 329.

BonJour wishes to argue that either the investigators have no such reasons, in which case their beliefs are not justified and we have been given no reason at all to believe the things they claim, or, alternatively, they do have such reasons, in which case reflection has played a crucial and ineliminable role in the evaluation in question. If BonJour is right about this, then the importance of reflective knowledge is secured.

So let us imagine one of these investigators making the case for a certain view about a psychological process as a result of a large body of experimental data, and let us suppose, as well, that this psychologist does not ever appeal to any first-person reflection on his own mental state. He simply presents the data, and makes an argument for a certain explanation of the data. Now the methods which the psychologist used, and the psychological processes which he underwent when evaluating the data, will have to be reliable if the claims which are made are to be worthy of our trust and belief. But BonJour wishes to ask whether the investigator, or anyone listening to him, has any reflective access to the fact—assuming it to be a fact—of their reliability.

> But if neither the investigator nor the audience have any [reflective] access to the fact of reliability or unreliability, it is impossible for any of them to tell which of these possibilities is actually realized.[36]

And if it is impossible for them to tell, BonJour argues, then neither the investigator nor his audience either know or justifiably believe anything at all about the results of the study. Without reflective access to reasons, neither knowledge nor justified belief is possible.

This looks to be a very powerful argument for the indispensability of reflective knowledge. So let us consider a belief of mine, say, the belief that p. And let us suppose, just to be charitable, that this belief of mine is reliably produced. Nevertheless, let us also suppose that I do not have reflective access to the process by which p was produced, nor do I have reflective access to the reliability of that process. Now BonJour says that if I don't have access to the reliability of the process—and access here means first-person introspective or reflective access—then it is impossible for me to tell whether the belief is reliably produced or not, and thus I can't really tell whether p is true, and so I have neither justified belief nor knowledge that p. But I don't see why 'being able to tell whether p is true' requires

---

[36] Ibid. 332. BonJour makes a similar argument in 'The Indispensability of Internalism', *Philosophical Topics*, 29 (2001), 47–65.

having this kind of reflective access to the reliability of the process by which the belief is produced. I can tell whether p is true if I am appropriately responsive to situations in which p is true. Nothing more than that is required. BonJour's suggestion that I 'can't tell' whether p is true makes it sound as if I'm in a very weak epistemic position. But notice that BonJour will insist that I can't tell whether p is true—in his sense—even in cases where I form the belief that p when and only when p is true (so long as I have no reflective access to the reliability of the process by which my belief is produced). Now this isn't what I mean when I say that someone can't tell whether p. I have in mind, instead, that such a person either is unable to form beliefs about whether p is true at all, or, if such beliefs are formed, they are very frequently wrong about whether p. Being unable to tell, in BonJour's sense, is compatible with having beliefs about p which are perfectly reliable. That doesn't sound so bad to me. Being in such a situation requires reliable connection with the world. I can understand why I would want that, and what I would be missing if I lacked it. There seems an important distinction here between people who do, and those who do not, have this kind of connection to the world.

What BonJour requires, however, is that, in order to justifiably believe that p, I must have reflective access to my reasons for believing that p. But as we have seen above in section 1.1, if we require this, then in order to justifiably believe that p, I need to have reflectively justified belief that I have certain reasons; and in order to be justified in believing that, I have to have reflective access to my reasons for believing it. And so on. An infinite regress results. The concept of justified belief to which BonJour appeals in showing the indispensability of reflection makes justified belief unattainable. It is hard to see why we should care about justified belief (or knowledge) so defined.

BonJour's argument for the indispensability of reflection thus turns on an account of justified belief and knowledge which make them necessarily unattainable. The fact that we lack both justified belief and knowledge in BonJour's sense, then, does not show something interesting about our cognitive situation. There is an important difference between those who are in a position to form beliefs about the world in a reliable manner and those who are not. It is clear why we should care about this difference.[37]

---

[37] This point serves to undermine another suggestion Sosa makes. In *Reflective Knowledge: Apt Belief and Reflective Knowledge*, ii. 142, Sosa suggests: 'What favors reflective over unreflective knowledge? Reflective acquisition of knowledge is, again, like attaining a prized

But it is entirely unclear why we should care about knowledge and justified belief as BonJour defines them. BonJour's attempt to defend the indispensability of reflection thus fails.

What then should we say about the other reasons offered for the importance of reflection? I will deal with each of these suggestions more briefly.

The point about skepticism is difficult to evaluate. Certainly as skepticism is traditionally presented, the only kind of solution that would be acceptable would be one which involved reflective knowledge. Indeed, something very much like BonJour's reflective requirement for knowledge, discussed in section 1.1, may be used to generate a skeptical argument. But it is difficult to see why this should count in favor of the importance of reflection rather than against that understanding of what knowledge amounts to. In addition, while it is certainly true that externalist accounts of knowledge and justification—accounts which do not make reflective assessment a requirement—seem to by-pass, rather than directly address traditional skepticism, we should not simply assume that this is a defect in these accounts, rather than a strength. So the appeal to the way in which only reflective knowledge would count as a solution to the traditional skeptical problem does not clearly show the importance of reflective knowledge.[38]

Sosa's final suggestion on behalf of reflection involves the idea that reflection is connected to epistemic agency. In the passage quoted above, Sosa remarks that 'we are unwilling to yield our intellectual autonomy'. He also remarks that 'reflection aids agency, control of conduct by the whole

objective guided by one's own intelligence, information, and deliberation; unreflective acquisition of knowledge is like lucking into some benefit in the dark.' But not only on the account suggested above, but on Sosa's own account, animal knowledge requires that one's belief be reliably produced. For that very reason, the truth of the belief which results from such a process can hardly be counted a matter of luck. This is nothing at all like accidentally acquiring some benefit in the dark. Moreover, the fact that animal knowledge does not involve reflection does not in any way suggest that the goal of true belief is not attained under the guidance of one's own intelligence and information. Both of these factors may play an important role in animal knowledge so long as reflection does not also play a role. The matter of deliberation is more complicated, and will be addressed in Ch. 2; it will also re-emerge, in the context of the discussion of choice rather than belief, in Ch. 3.

[38] There are other reasons for worrying about the extent to which reflective knowledge, at least as Sosa now defines it (see n. 8 above), can aid in the project of defending against the skeptic. If reflective knowledge is just apt belief aptly noted, then it seems that reflective knowledge need put the reflective knower in no more position to defend his or her own belief (against skepticism, or against even against more modest challenges) than the animal knower.

person, not just by peripheral modules'.[39] The thought here is that, when we arrive at beliefs unreflectively, our beliefs are arrived at passively. They are not, then, attributable to us. Believing in this case is not something that we do; it is something that happens to us. When we reflect, however, our beliefs are under our control. They are no longer merely passively arrived at; they are our doing. And to the extent that we value our intellectual autonomy, then, we will value reflectively arrived at belief.

The topic of epistemic agency and intellectual autonomy is a large one, and we will need to discuss it in detail. We will turn to it in Chapter 3. But we need not deal with it here in order to see that this defense of reflective knowledge cannot carry the day.

Consider an analogy. It is well known that, if one is traveling some large distance from one city to another, it is far safer to take a commercial airliner than it is to drive. The fatality rate per passenger mile is far, far higher for driving, as is the injury rate. In spite of this, many people continue to express safety concerns about flying in these situations, and, because of this, often prefer to drive. When these people are confronted with the safety statistics, one is sometimes offered the following justification: 'Yes, I know that's what the statistics show, but I prefer to be in control.'

It's hard to know how to interpret this response. Certainly, when I fly on a commercial airplane, I'm quite pleased that it is the pilot, and not I, who controls the plane, especially since I have no experience as a pilot. I'm more than happy to cede my autonomy in such a situation. Now perhaps the people who offer this response care a good deal more about control than I do. I want to arrive at my destination safely, and if ceding control is the best way to do that, then that is fine with me. But for someone who values their autonomy highly, it will be important to consider the tradeoff between safety and autonomy. Even so, given the very large differences in safety between driving and flying, one would have to value autonomy a great deal to make it reasonable to choose to drive rather than fly.

The situation is quite similar with respect to intellectual autonomy. We all, I believe, have very good reason to care about the truth of our beliefs. Whatever it is that we care about, we will more likely be able to act in ways which allow us to achieve it if our beliefs are true.[40] Now some people also care about intellectual autonomy. They want to be in control

---

[39] 'Replies', 292.
[40] I have argued for this at length in *Knowledge and its Place in Nature*, ch. 5.

of their intellectual processes and to form beliefs in ways which are, in some important sense, under their control. If having control of one's belief-forming processes aided in the project of having more accurate beliefs, then this desire for intellectual autonomy would not only fail to conflict with the goal of having true beliefs; it would positively aid in achieving that goal. But as we have seen above, there is reason to believe that reflective belief acquisition does not, in general, have this beneficial effect. There are times, to be sure, when reflective belief acquisition can serve to correct mistakes which we would otherwise make. But there is a large class of cases in which it does not do this, and there are many cases where reflection actually impairs our accuracy.[41] So we do not find ourselves in the fortunate position where a desire for control over our intellectual faculties, and a desire for accurate belief, are perfectly complementary. As in the case of safety and control when it comes to the decision whether to fly or to drive, tradeoffs will need to be made. And given the effects which reflection actually produces, one will have to value intellectual autonomy a great deal if one is to prefer, in general, reflectively arrived at belief to belief which is arrived at unreflectively.

Indeed, from an epistemological point of view, it is very hard to see why we should value intellectual autonomy for itself. Consider some of the perceptual processes we undergo unreflectively. Many of these are extremely reliable in producing accurate beliefs about the environment. If we take the view which Sosa suggests in the passages quoted above, there is something valuable missing in beliefs formed in this way, since, by failing to reflect, we fail to act autonomously; indeed, we fail to act at all. So imagine for a moment that we could have intellectual faculties which were even more reliable than our perceptual faculties; imagine that we could have belief producing mechanisms which were perfectly reliable. More than this, imagine that these mechanisms might operate in us unreflectively. We simply pick up information about the world in a perfectly reliable manner without having to reflectively monitor our belief acquisition at all. Would we be missing out on something valuable here insofar as we fail to reflect and thereby assert our autonomy? Would reflection be valuable, in such a situation, even if it compromised our reliability? From an epistemological point of view, I cannot see why it

---

[41] On this last point, see e.g. Halberstadt and Wilson, 'Reflections on Conscious Reflection: Mechanisms of Impairment by Reasons Analysis', 557–61.

would. Perhaps autonomy is a valuable thing that we should care about in its own right, but if it is, I cannot see why we should think of it as epistemically valuable.

From an epistemological point of view, we should value reflection to the extent that, and only to the extent that, it contributes to our reliability. The appeal to the value of autonomy either presupposes, what is not true, that reflective belief acquisition is likely to be more reliable than unreflective belief acquisition, or it is simply an appeal to some sort of extra-epistemic value. Epistemologically speaking, there is no reason to value reflectively arrived at belief in general over unreflective belief.

1.5 Reflection and the first-person point of view

Many philosophers have the conviction that the most fundamental questions of epistemology are, at bottom, questions that must be asked from the first-person point of view, and, to the extent that they are convinced of this, they will see reflection as essential to justification and knowledge. Thus, for example, Richard Foley argues that a particularly fundamental question for epistemology is 'What am I to believe?' and although he acknowledges that there is a way to answer such a question from a third-person perspective, by, for example, engaging in psychological research about the reliability of one's own processes of belief acquisition, such an investigation would not approach this question in the way that treats it as the fundamental epistemological question he has in mind. The approach he favors, one which respects the fundamental nature of the question, is as follows.

I am to make up my mind by marshaling my intellectual resources in a way that conforms to my own deepest standards. If I conduct my inquiries in such a way that I would not be critical of the resulting beliefs even if I were to be deeply reflective, then these beliefs are rational for me in an important sense, an egoistic sense.... The basic idea is that if I am to be egoistically rational, I must not have internal reasons for retraction, ones whose force I myself would acknowledge were I to be sufficiently reflective.[42]

---

[42] 'What Am I to Believe?', in Steven Wagner and Richard Warner (eds), *Naturalism: A Critical Appraisal* (University of Notre Dame Press, 1993), 148.

So reflection plays an essential role in addressing a fundamental epistemo-logical issue, and any attempt to answer a question which sounds like Foley's, by third-person means, simply fails to get at the issue about which he is concerned.

Laurence BonJour says something quite similar. Although he allows that there may be a perfectly legitimate externalist notion of justification, and of knowledge—and that accounts of these notions would make no special appeal to the first-person perspective or to reflection—nevertheless, there is also a legitimate internalist notion of justification, and a notion of knowledge which requires such justification. Such a notion requires that 'what is appealed to for justification must be *internal to the individual's first-person cognitive perspective*'.[43] Moreover, BonJour insists, these two notions of justification, and of knowledge, are not on a par.

I want to insist that there is a clear way in which an internalist approach, in addition to being intellectually legitimate on its own, has a fundamental kind of priority for epistemology as a whole.[44]

So for both Foley and BonJour, there are fundamental questions about what we ourselves should believe, and the most fundamental way to pursue such questions must itself be from the first-person perspective. This will inevitably involve reflecting on our beliefs, and their sources, and the relationship among them. In order to answer the fundamental questions of epistemology, reflection will need to play a leading role.

Debates about which questions in a discipline are really the most funda-mental can often seem terribly unproductive, with members of each side of the debate doing little more than insisting that it is their preferred approach which really gets to the bottom of things. But that is not the case here. There are arguments for the priority of the first-person perspective, and if these arguments are successful, then justification and knowledge will inevitably involve reflection. Let us look at how these arguments play out.

While some internalist epistemologists characterize internalism by way of a metaphysical distinction—e.g. that the justificatory status of a person's beliefs depends exclusively on states of the person which are, in some suitable sense, internal (in the way that, say, mental states are)[45]—BonJour

---

[43] 'Indispensability of Internalism', 54.   [44] Ibid. 62.

[45] This is the way that Conee and Feldman characterize internalism. See *Evidentialism: Essays in Epistemology* (Oxford University Press, 2004), 56: 'The justificatory status of a person's doxastic attitudes strongly supervenes on the person's occurrent and dispositional

rightly rejects this way of thinking about internalism. While it is certainly true that for Descartes, as clear a case of an internalist epistemologist as one might try to find, the justificatory status of a person's belief did have to supervene on features of that person's mental state, this is only because Descartes held a view which made this metaphysical distinction—the distinction between things internal to the mind and those external to it in the physical world—correspond to an important epistemological distinction: namely, the distinction between those things which are known directly and with certainty, as opposed to those things which are known only indirectly and fallibly. For those who reject the claim that the metaphysical distinction between mental and non-mental items tracks this epistemological divide—as everyone now must—it must therefore be acknowledged that the metaphysical distinction does not capture, and is not even extensionally equivalent to, any epistemological distinction at all. There are some mental states, such as the early states of perceptual and linguistic processing—to which our epistemological access is extraordinarily indirect.[46] We have far better cognitive access to many states of the so-called external world than we do to some of the states of our own psychology. And, finally, even mental states to which we seem to have some sort of direct access which would license claims about certainty turn out, on further examination (of the sort discussed in section 1.3), not to answer to that description. When internalists talk about things internal to us, they need to have an epistemological notion in mind rather than a metaphysical one.

What is this epistemological notion of the internal, a notion which will illuminate the fundamental nature of the question both Foley and BonJour wish to address? BonJour, I believe, is especially helpful here.

A person's conscious mental states play the role that they standardly do in internalist conceptions of justification, I would suggest, *not* simply because they are internal to him or her in the sense merely of being his or her individual states, but rather because it is arguable that some (but not all) of the properties of such states, mainly

mental states, events, and conditions.' In saying this, I do not mean to be endorsing the view that mental states are 'internal'. This is not my view. It is the view of certain kinds of internalist. Any such view, I believe, comes with substantial theoretical commitments of a sort I would reject.

[46] This is going to be so on any way that one tries to make sense of the direct/indirect distinction. I do not mean to be endorsing any particular way of making out such a distinction, or, indeed, even the claim that we can make good sense of it.

their specific content and the attitude toward that content that they reflect, are things to which the person has a first-person access that is direct and unproblematic, that is, that does not depend on other claims that would themselves have to be justified in some more indirect way.[47]

BonJour thus rightly gives an epistemological characterization of the features which make an internal state internal: it must be a state to which one has 'first-person access that is direct and unproblematic'. Internalism is thus defined in terms which assure the importance of reflection, for first-person access here just is the sort of access that reflection affords.

Why should we think, however, that reflection affords access which is unproblematic? It is clear enough that, when we reflect, the access which reflection affords us to various features of our mental life certainly *seems* unproblematic from the first-person perspective. What reason do we have, however, for taking such appearances at face value?

Notice, first of all, the context in which BonJour speaks of our access to certain features of our mental life[48] as unproblematic. BonJour comes to talk about unproblematic access in the context of raising the problem of radical skepticism.[49] The same is true of Foley; his question about what one is to believe is presented, unsurprisingly, as a distinctively Cartesian question, one which serves to make vivid the problem of skepticism. And Sosa too, as we have seen, sees an important connection between the importance of reflective knowledge and the traditional project of responding to the skeptic.[50] So how is it that our access to certain features of our mental life is supposed to be unproblematic in the context of responding to radical skepticism?

There is no denying that one can raise a skeptical challenge to knowledge of the physical world by granting, for the sake of argument, that we

---

[47] 'Indispensability of Internalism', 54.

[48] And various extra-mental items as well. BonJour rightly points out that, on standard internalist accounts, we have such unproblematic access by way of reflection to at least some a priori knowable truths. Ibid. 55. I will focus in the text, however, on our access to relevant features of our mental lives. If internalists cannot secure this, then internalism is committed to an extremely broad skepticism, and, indeed, the coherence of the entire position is threatened. More than this, there is every reason to believe that the kind of argument I make against unproblematic access to mental items can easily be generalized to cover the cases in which BonJour believes we have unproblematic access to a priori knowable truths. I have discussed these problems about the a priori in 'The Impurity of Reason', *Pacific Philosophical Quarterly*, 81 (2000), 67–89. It would take us too far afield from the issues under discussion here to pursue these questions about the a priori.

[49] 'Indispensability of Internalism', 53.

[50] 'Replies', 292.

have perfect access to (at least some features of) our mental states. We can raise skeptical challenges of all sorts, by granting, for the sake of argument, that certain sorts of knowledge are unproblematic. Thus, for example, we might grant, for the sake of argument, that we have unproblematic knowledge of the behavior of others, and then ask, in the light of this knowledge, how knowledge of their mental states is possible. Or we might grant, again, for the sake of argument, that knowledge of the observable features of the world is unproblematic, and then ask how knowledge of unobservables is possible. We can raise all sorts of skeptical challenges in this way. When we do so, however, the knowledge that we take as unproblematic is not, automatically, unproblematic *tout court*. At least without additional argument, to say that a certain body of knowledge is unproblematic for the purposes of raising a skeptical problem is simply to allow that, within a certain dialectical situation, we are not going to raise challenges to that sort of knowledge. But this shows nothing at all about the epistemic status of the knowledge which we agree not to challenge. What BonJour, and Foley, and Sosa need to show, if they are to secure the importance of the first-person perspective, and the importance of reflective knowledge which goes with it, is that our first-person access to relevant features of our mental life is unproblematic in a far more substantive way.

But this is just what they cannot do. One can raise skeptical worries about features of one's mental life just as easily as one can raise worries about our knowledge of the physical world. Descartes prepared the ground for skepticism about the physical world by, initially, pointing out that we do in fact make mistakes about various features of the external world. This is enough to show that there is not only in principle, but, at times, in practice as well, a gap between how the world actually is and how we represent it in our beliefs. This is all that is needed to generate the skeptical worry: what reason is there to believe that the world is anything like the way we represent it to be?

But the very same strategy will generate a skeptical worry about our access to our mental states. The experiments reviewed in section 1.3 show that there is not only in principle, but, at times, in practice as well, a gap between how our mental life actually is and how it is presented to us when we reflect. Considerations of cases involving self-deception show that we may, at times, be mistaken about what it is that we believe, so here too, there is, not only in theory, but in practice as well, a non-trivial gap between appearance and reality. And it is the possibility of such a gap

REFLECTION AND THE FIRST-PERSON POINT OF VIEW 39

which raises the skeptical worry: what reason is there to believe that our mental life is anything like the way it appears to us when we reflect on it?

I am not, in any way, a radical skeptic. These considerations are not meant to provide support for radical skepticism. What they do show, however, is that the sense in which the beliefs about our mental life which are generated from the first-person perspective—that is, the beliefs which result from reflection—are not unproblematic in any way that matters to epistemology.[51]

The idea that the first-person point of view presents some sort of neutral and unproblematic starting point for epistemological inquiry is, to my mind, a product of two not unrelated facts. First, there is an important historical tradition in epistemology, a tradition of which Descartes is the preeminent representative, according to which the way the mind is presented to us in reflection genuinely is unproblematic: it is unproblematic because it is absolutely certain and utterly resistant to any sort of skeptical doubt whatsoever. Second, there is the psychological fact that, when we do reflect on our own mental states, we are presented with a view of our mental life which we tend to find utterly compelling. Neither of these facts, however, should convince us that the access to our mental life which reflection provides and which is represented in our first-person perspective on our mental lives genuinely is unproblematic. Descartes's views about the powers of reflection are, for very good reason, no longer accepted, and without them, the claim that reflection provides an unproblematic view of our mental life is wholly undermined. The psychological fact about the compelling nature of the first-person perspective is itself put in proper perspective by the surprising experimental results which we have surveyed. Viewed in this light, there is nothing epistemically unproblematic about the first-person perspective or the epistemological projects which flow from treating it as if it were.

---

[51] BonJour seems to come quite close to acknowledging this. At one point he remarks that, 'Certainly it would be a very unusual brand of scepticism which would challenge whether my belief that B is justified by raising the issue of whether I do in fact accept B, the normal sceptical claim being precisely that certain beliefs which are in fact held are nonetheless unjustified.' (*The Structure of Empirical Knowledge*, 81.) But claims about which skeptical challenges are common in the history of philosophy, or which are unusual, tells us nothing about which kinds of claims are unproblematic *tout court*. And it is this sense of what is unproblematic, rather than the dialectical sense, which is epistemologically relevant.

1.6 Conclusion

There is something very tempting about the claim that genuine knowledge and justified belief require reflection. Indeed, we may be tempted by an extremely uncompromising version of this claim: any belief which is accepted in an unreflective manner is itself unjustified. As we have seen, such a claim quickly generates an infinite regress. What seemed like a high standard for justification, but a perfectly reasonable one nonetheless, turns out on closer examination to present us with unreasonable and unrealizable ideals.

There is a way, however, of preserving the intuition that there is something special about reflection, and that knowledge which involves reflection is especially to be prized. We may draw a distinction between two sorts of knowledge—one which requires reflection and one which does not—and, if we do this in the right sort of way, we may avoid the infinite regress. But it won't do simply to show that such a distinction is coherent. We must also show that it is well motivated. There is, to be sure, a commonsensical motivation for such a distinction in the thought that by reflecting on the epistemic credentials of our beliefs, we thereby subject them to a higher level of scrutiny than belief unreflectively acquired. It turns out, however, that this commonsensical view presupposes certain empirical claims about the reliability of reflective scrutiny, claims which, surprisingly, turn out to be false. The main motivation for drawing a distinction between reflective and unreflective knowledge is thereby undermined. We have examined a number of alternative motivations, and found that these motivations as well cannot bear the weight of the tempting distinction. It seems that there really is no ground at all for drawing a distinction between unreflective knowledge and something better, knowledge which involves reflection.

We examined one further attempt to explain the special place of reflective knowledge in epistemology, one which grounds it in the first-person perspective. But, perhaps unsurprisingly, any such attempt inevitably falls to the problems which beset the simple commonsensical defense of the distinction. From an epistemological point of view, there is nothing special about the first-person perspective which can provide a defense of the distinction between reflective and unreflective knowledge.

Just to be clear: I do not hold the absurd view that we should never reflect on our beliefs and their epistemic status. It would be no more reasonable to hold this than it would be to hold that reflecting on our beliefs can cure all the ills that might beset belief unreflectively arrived at. What we should value, instead, is reliably acquired belief, whether it is acquired with or without the aid of reflection. And this is just to say that when it comes to belief acquisition and retention, reflection is just one[52] more process among others, to be evaluated in just the same way as any other.

---

[52] Actually, it is, of course, more than just one process, and a full evaluation of it will require understanding all of the different processes which comprise it.

2

Reasoning

What is reasoning? What is involved when we form a belief on the basis of reasons? Let us consider a simple example. Once again, I'm listening to the radio, and this time I hear the weather forecaster announce that rain is likely this afternoon. I know that I have a class in the afternoon on a distant corner of campus, and so I conclude that, if I don't want to get wet, I'd better bring an umbrella with me when I leave home. My reason for believing that I ought to bring an umbrella to work is just my belief that rain is likely later in the day. But insofar as this is my reason for belief, what must the relationship be between my belief that rain is likely and my belief that I should bring an umbrella?

One natural thought here is that the relationship must be causal: my belief that rain is likely must have been at least part of what caused me to believe that I should bring an umbrella if it is to be even part of my reason for that belief. If my belief that I should bring an umbrella was somehow triggered in me by something other than my coming to believe that rain is likely—for example, if I had come to believe that I should bring an umbrella because I wanted to show off my fancy new umbrella to a friend—then my belief that it is going to rain would not have been my reason for believing that I should take an umbrella. If I am to reason from one belief to another—if the first belief is to be part of my reason for believing the second—then the first belief must have played some causal role in producing (or sustaining) the second belief.

But surely this is not enough. There are, after all, lots of ways in which one belief might play a role in producing or sustaining a second belief which would not constitute either reasoning or believing for a reason. Suppose I hear some shocking news—perhaps that some terrible event has occurred—and this causes me to drop my coffee cup. My believing that the terrible event occurred played a causal role then in causing me to drop my cup; and that, in turn, caused me to believe that I had dropped my cup.

But this is not to say that my believing that the terrible event had occurred was my reason, or any part of my reason, for believing that I had dropped my cup. One belief may cause another, or play a causal role in producing another, without serving as a reason for the second belief.

So what else is required if one belief is to be one's reason, or part of one's reason, for holding a second? One suggestion that some philosophers have found attractive is this: one must believe that the first belief provides one with a good reason for believing the second. Without such a belief, the relationship between the first and second belief may be causal without the first being one's reason for believing the second. In order for one belief to be one's reason for another, one must regard it as a reason, and this means that one must have the belief that the first belief is a reason for holding the second. Reasoning, on such a view, thus requires a second-order belief. Where do such beliefs come from? They have their origins in reflection. By reflecting on our first-order beliefs, we may come to have second-order beliefs about our reasons.

In this chapter, we will examine views which make second-order beliefs about reasons a necessary condition for reasoning.

2.1 The infinite regress

Consider, then, what Sydney Shoemaker says about rational change of belief and rational change of desire.

I agree that we don't need any self-awareness in order to explain why beliefs and desires jointly produce effects which they rationalize—i.e., actions which it is rational for the subject of such a set of desires to perform. Given that the agent is rational, the mere existence of such beliefs and desires is sufficient to explain their having the appropriate effects. But if the beliefs and desires are all first-order beliefs and desires, i.e., beliefs and desires that are not themselves *about* the agent's beliefs and desires, then one thing they do not rationalize is changes in themselves. For such changes to be rationalized, the beliefs and desires would have to include second-order beliefs and desires—desires to promote consistency and coherence in the system of beliefs and desires, and beliefs about what changes in the beliefs and desires would be needed in order to satisfy the second-order desires, which in turn would require beliefs about what the current beliefs and desires are.[1]

---

[1] 'On Knowing One's Own Mind', repr. in *The First-Person Perspective and Other Essays* (Cambridge University Press, 1996), 32–3.

So on Shoemaker's view, a person cannot rationally change his beliefs or desires without first knowing what they are, desiring to promote consistency and coherence in his or her beliefs or desires, and then changing them on the basis of that very desire. First-order beliefs and desires alone will not do; second-order mental states are needed for rational change of both belief and desire.

Shoemaker is not alone in holding such a view. Thus, Michael Williams insists that reasoning requires sensitivity to reasons. But this, in turn, according to Williams, requires second-order belief.

To become sensitive to reasons is to learn what can and cannot reasonably be questioned, and why. Thus acquiring sensitivity to reasons requires a lot of know-how, as well as extensive meta-knowledge.[2]

Meta-knowledge, of course, is just second-order knowledge; it is knowledge about one's beliefs. If one is to be capable of reasoning at all, according to Williams, one must have a good deal of second-order knowledge. As Williams sees it, having beliefs requires being sensitive to reasons; being sensitive to reasons requires epistemic responsibility; epistemic responsibility requires attentiveness to one's capacities, strengths and weaknesses, abilities and limitations; and this, in turn, requires beliefs about one's own beliefs. We might put this view in the form of a slogan: No cognition without meta-cognition. This is a way of looking at things which Williams explicitly endorses, and, as he points out, he has a good deal of company in viewing things in this way:

the main point...has to do with whether knowledge of the environment is essentially bound up with...'meta-cognitive processing'. Brandom, Davidson and I all think that it is.[3]

---

[2] 'Is Knowledge a Natural Phenomenon?', in Schantz (2004: 208).

[3] Ibid. 194. For the other authors Williams cites, see Robert Brandom, *Making it Explicit: Reasoning, Representing and Discursive Commitment* (Harvard University Press, 1994), and *Articulating Reasons: An Introduction to Inferentialism* (Harvard University Press, 2000), especially essay 3: 'Insights and Blindspots of Reliabilism'; Donald Davidson, especially 'Thought and Talk', repr. in *Inquiries into Truth and Interpretation* (Oxford University Press, 1984), 155–70, and 'Rational Animals', repr. in *Subjective, Intersubjective, Objective* (Oxford University Press, 2001), 95–105. Two more authors with related views are John Haugeland, *Having Thought: Essays in the Metaphysics of Mind* (Harvard University Press, 1998), and John McDowell, *Mind and World* (Harvard University Press, 1996). Although there are important differences among their views, Brandom, Haugeland, McDowell, and Williams are all heavily influenced on these issues by Wilfrid Sellars, *Science, Perception, and Reality* (Routledge & Kegan Paul, 1963), especially essay 5: 'Empiricism and the Philosophy of Mind'.

Each of these views will require a good deal of scrutiny. We may begin, however, by pointing out one pitfall which they all must avoid: the infinite regress.

As I pointed out in the Introduction, one particularly simple version of the view that reasoning requires second-order beliefs about reasons leads straightforwardly to an infinite regress. If one holds that my belief that p can only be my reason for believing that q if I also believe that believing that p is a reason for believing that q, then trouble is just around the corner. This belief about reasons must surely play a role in my reasoning, for the whole point of this account is to distinguish between cases in which one merely has a belief that plays no such role, and the cases in which beliefs are genuinely involved in reasoning. If the higher order belief is merely a by-stander to reasoning, it cannot do the work of distinguishing between genuine cases of reasoning and cases in which one has a reason but is not moved by it. But once the second-order belief about reasons must itself play an active role in reasoning, the requirement that reasoning involve a higher-order appreciation of one's reasons comes into play yet again. So now one needs a (third-order) belief about one's second-order belief in order for that second-order belief to play an active role in reasoning, and so on. One is launched on an infinite regress. The apparently innocent requirement that reasoning involves a higher-order appreciation of one's reasons is thereby shown to be untenable.

We will need to see whether proponents of the view that reasoning requires some sort of second-order belief can avoid such an infinite regress, and, if so, how they do so. And we will also need to see whether the requirement of some sort of meta-cognition if reasoning is to take place is itself a reasonable one, assuming it can be presented in a way which avoids the regress problem. So let us turn to these issues.

2.2 Shoemaker's higher-order requirement

Let us return to Shoemaker's view. Someone might hold that rational action is not possible without some sort of second-order endorsement: one cannot act rationally, on such a view, without recognizing that one has a certain belief and a certain desire, and, at the same time, wanting to act in a way which satisfies one's desires given the way one takes the world to be. But Shoemaker does not hold any such view. He recognizes that this would over-intellectualize rational action. Ben acts rationally when he, without reflecting on his beliefs or desires at all, makes a complicated series of turns in the course of his drive home at the end of the day. Ben has done this often enough that he need not think about the route home; he certainly doesn't need to think about what he wants—to get home—or his beliefs about how to get there, or whether acting on the basis of his desire to get home, given how he takes the world to be, is most likely to satisfy his desire. Ben, like most of us at the end of a long day, just gets in the car and drives. But his action is no less rational for that. And Shoemaker would not have it any other way.

So why does Shoemaker think that things are any different when it comes to rational change of belief? Ben believed, when he first got into the car, that he could get home by turning left on Main Street. When he got to Main Street, however, he found that there was construction blocking the route. Seeing the construction had the effect of changing his belief about how he might get home: he no longer believed that turning left on Main would do the trick. Is Ben's change in belief rational only if he also, first, thinks about what he believes, and second, thinks about his desire for consistent and coherent belief, and finally, in light of all of this, changes his beliefs in light of the previous reflections? If this is what rational belief change requires, it seems that most of our belief changes are not rational for we rarely go through such an elaborate and explicit process of reasoning. Rather, our beliefs often change in response to reasons without the intervention of second-order mental states. But there seems no more reason to insist on the intervention of second-order beliefs and desires here than there is in the case of rational actions of other sorts.

Shoemaker is aware of this sort of problem. In response, he argues, first, that rational individuals behave *as if* they have the relevant second-order beliefs and desires:

In a rational being, there are two sorts of causal efficacy exerted by the first-order beliefs and desires. They jointly produce such effects as their contents make it rational for them to produce. And they jointly produce such effects as are needed in order to preserve or promote consistency and coherence in the belief-desire system. The latter may require the initiation of investigations aimed at discovering which of two inconsistent propositions is true, and of reasoning aimed at discovering which of two such propositions coheres best with certain other propositions, which are the contents of the beliefs that are part of the system. Now it seems to me that the least we can say of this case is that it is *as if* the system contained a desire to be a rational and coherent belief-desire system, and beliefs (true beliefs) about what beliefs and desires it contains.[4]

Let us grant, for the sake of argument then, that Ben behaves as if he desires to be rational and as if he knows what he wants and believes. Even so, one might still think that there will be cases in which such behavior is actually accompanied by second-order beliefs and desires of this sort, and there are cases, many of them, which are not so accompanied. Even the latter, it seems, involve rational change of belief.

But Shoemaker denies this.

I am tempted to say that if everything is as *if* a creature has knowledge of its beliefs and desires, then it *does* have knowledge of them. There is no phenomenology of self-knowledge of such states that is in danger of being ignored if we say this— there is nothing it is like to believe something, and there need not be anything it is like to know or believe that one believes something. What I am inclined to say is that second-order belief, and the knowledge it typically embodies, is supervenient on first order beliefs and desires—or rather, it is supervenient on these plus a certain degree of rationality, intelligence, and conceptual capacity. By this I mean that one has the former *in* having the latter—that having the former is nothing over and above having the latter.[5]

So Shoemaker has a distinctive view about the metaphysics of second- and higher-order belief. One might have thought that the belief that p and the belief that one believes that p are as distinct from one another as the belief that p and the belief that q. But Shoemaker does not accept such a view. On Shoemaker's view, having the second-order belief that one believes that p is in part constituted by one's first-order belief that p. While the belief that q is wholly distinct from the belief that p, in most cases, the belief that one believes that p is intimately connected to the first-order belief that p. On Shoemaker's view, when one comes to believe that p, in so doing, one acquires the second-order belief that one believes that p as well.

Precisely because Shoemaker has these distinctive views about the metaphysics of higher-order belief, the threat of the regress seems to be blunted. If rational change of belief required an infinite hierarchy of beliefs, and each of these beliefs were as independent of one another as the belief that p is from the belief that q, then the infinite regress would pose an insurmountable problem. But since Shoemaker holds that

[4] 'On Knowing One's Own Mind', 33.   [5] Ibid. 34.

higher-order beliefs are acquired in virtue of acquiring the first-order belief—since one gets the higher-order belief for free, as it were—the regress seems to be harmless.

Notice that Shoemaker does not say that second-order belief is supervenient on first-order belief alone. This is important because there are many creatures, such as non-human animals and very young children, who have first-order beliefs but clearly do not have any second-order beliefs at all.[6] Indeed, non-human animals and infants do not even have the concept of belief, and without any such concept, they cannot have beliefs about the beliefs they have.[7] Thus, on Shoemaker's view, merely having a belief that p does not entail that one also have the belief that one has the belief that p. The second-order belief supervenes on the first-order belief 'plus a certain degree of rationality, intelligence, and conceptual capacity'. So infants and non-human animals, who lack the concept of belief, therefore do not have second-order beliefs. Higher-order beliefs do not come entirely for free.

Once we acknowledge this, however, the regress is no longer avoided. I do, admittedly, have the concept of second-order belief; I'm that conceptually sophisticated. I can also conceive of beliefs about my beliefs about my beliefs; I thereby, on Shoemaker's view, have third-order beliefs. But it is not at all clear that I can form the concept of beliefs of arbitrarily high order. And if I cannot, then I will have some highest-order belief which is not backed by a belief of still higher order. If rational belief change requires having higher-order beliefs all the way up, as Shoemaker's requirement seems to entail, we no longer have a solution to the regress problem.

Even leaving the regress aside, however, there are other difficulties which Shoemaker's view encounters. Why should the having of a

---

[6] Shoemaker simply (and plausibly, to my mind) assumes this, but there is a good deal of empirical literature in support of such a claim. See n. 7 below.

[7] Children do not acquire the concept of belief, and so do not have beliefs about beliefs, until approximately age 4 and a half. See e.g. Janet Wilde Astington, *The Child's Discovery of the Mind* (Harvard University Press, 1993). In the case of non-human animals, the best candidates for having higher-order beliefs are apes, but there is substantial reason to be cautious about suggesting that they do, in fact, have such beliefs. See Daniel Povinelli and T. J. Eddy, 'What Young Chimpanzees Know about Seeing', *Monographs of the Society for Research in Child Development*, 61 (1996), 1–152; Michael Tomasello and Josep Call, *Primate Cognition* (Oxford University Press, 1997). For a somewhat more optimistic assessment, see Michael Tomasello, 'Chimpanzees Understand Psychological States: The Question is Which Ones and to What Extent', *Trends in Cognitive Science*, 7 (2003), 153–6.

first-order belief, together with rationality, intelligence, and relevant conceptual capacities, automatically bring second-order belief in its train? We have many capacities which we do not exercise. Surely it is possible to have certain conceptual and intellectual capacities without bringing them to bear wherever they might apply. It may well be that if Ben were to focus his attention on the question of what it is that he believes, the fact that he does believe that p, together with his intellectual and conceptual capacities, would guarantee, or at least make it likely, that he come to recognize that he believes that p. This does not mean, however, that second-order belief supervenes on first-order belief plus these various capacities. If the capacities are not exercised, no second-order beliefs will result. So there is no reason to deny that Ben might change his beliefs even without having any sort of second-order belief about those changes. And there is no reason to deny that when that happens, the resulting changes are rational.

Indeed, once Shoemaker allows that second-order beliefs do not supervene on first-order beliefs alone, as he must, the claim that rational belief change requires higher-order belief is undermined. Creatures who lack the concept of belief surely change their beliefs in response to evidence. Just as Ben stops believing that he can get home by turning left on Main Street even without having first to form beliefs about his beliefs, an infant child will stop believing that Ben is in front of him as soon as Ben leaves the room even without forming any beliefs about what beliefs he has, let alone forming any sort of desire for coherent or consistent belief. Ben's dog is much the same. Its beliefs too are responsive to changes in its environment. Once we allow, as Shoemaker does, that Ben may act rationally without any intervening second-order beliefs or desires, and that an infant child and a dog may do so as well, it is very hard to see why we should insist that these changes in belief without the benefit of second-order belief are any less rational.

Rational belief change is nothing more than belief change which is responsive to reason. While such responsiveness may be achieved, at times, by way of reflection on one's beliefs and desires, it does not require any such reflection. If first-order beliefs, by themselves, were incapable of being responsive, in rational ways, to the presence of reasons, adding second-order beliefs surely wouldn't help. What special feature is it that second-order beliefs might have, and yet first-order beliefs must inevitably lack, that could allow beliefs to be reason-responsive only under the supervision, as it were, of higher-order belief? There is no special reason-adhering glue which is available only for beliefs of higher order. If first-order beliefs by themselves could not be responsive to reason, adding second-order beliefs wouldn't make the situation any better. But if first-order beliefs, by themselves, can be responsive to reason, as it surely seems they can, then second-order belief is not necessary for rational belief change.

2.3   Another route to a higher-order requirement

If Shoemaker's non-standard metaphysics of higher-order belief does not help to motivate a higher-order requirement on rational belief change, perhaps there is some other more promising route. We seem to find such a route in the work of Brandom, Davidson, Haugeland, McDowell, Sellars, and Williams. There are important differences among these authors, to be sure, but there is, I believe, a common thread among them which supports some sort of higher-order requirement on rational change of belief. Indeed, as we shall see, these authors all hold the surprising view that one cannot have any beliefs at all unless one has higher-order beliefs. We will thus need to begin by raising an issue about belief itself. What does it take for an individual to be capable of having beliefs? Let us consider three different types of individual.

First, consider the case of plants, which respond differentially to their environment: when sunlight is present, they turn toward it. Sunlight affects the plants in a way which brings about this motion, and it brings it about by bringing about various changes inside the plant. Internal states of the plant are thus reliably correlated with the presence of sunshine, and we may thus speak of these states as 'information-bearing states', but they are information-bearing in the very same sense that the internal states of my thermostat bear information about the temperature in my living room or the color of a strip of litmus paper bears information about the acidity of a sample of liquid. These states are stimulus-bound: individuals whose states are information-bearing in only this sense are predictable by way of stimulus-response connections alone. The frog's response to flies is like this.[8] If one rolls a piece of birdshot (BB) in front of the frog, it will suck it up as if it were a fly. Well, we all make mistakes. But the frog will do it a

---

[8] J. Y. Lettvin et al., 'What the Frog's Eye Tells the Frog's Brain', in Warren McCulloch, *Embodiments of Mind* (MIT Press, 1965), 230–55.

second time if a second BB is rolled in front of it; and a third; and a fourth; and so on. The frog will not learn from its experience. Receptors on the frog's retina are directly wired to states which produce the tongue-flicking response. The state which bears the information that there is a fly in front of the frog is not informationally integrated with other information the frog possesses. Similarly, as Dean Wooldridge notes:[9]

When the time comes for egg laying, the wasp *Sphex* builds a burrow for the purpose and seeks out a cricket which she stings in such a way as to paralyze but not kill it. She drags the cricket into the burrow, lays her eggs alongside, closes the burrow, then flies away, never to return. In due course, the eggs hatch and the wasp grubs feed off the paralyzed cricket, which has not decayed, having been kept in the wasp equivalent of deep freeze. To the human mind, such an elaborately organized and seemingly purposeful routine conveys a convincing flavor of logic and thoughtfulness—until more details are examined. For example, the Wasp's routine is to bring the paralyzed cricket to the burrow, leave it on the threshold, go inside to see that all is well, emerge, and then drag the cricket in. If the cricket is moved a few inches away while the wasp is inside making her preliminary inspection, the wasp, on emerging from the burrow, will bring the cricket back to the threshold, but not inside, and will then repeat the preparatory procedure of entering the burrow to see that everything is all right. If again the cricket is removed a few inches while the wasp is inside, once again she will move the cricket up to the threshold and re-enter the burrow for a final check. The wasp never thinks of pulling the cricket straight in. On one occasion this procedure was repeated forty times, always with the same result.

Individuals whose information-bearing states are all of this sort are exceptionally crude: they include various simple mechanical devices, plants, and such animals as paramecia.

But many animals are not like this. Their behavior is not explicable by way of simple stimulus–response connections. Thus, consider the piping plover, a bird which feigns a broken wing when a potential predator approaches its nest.[10] The bird moves away from the nest, thereby distracting the predator, and once the predator is far enough away from the nest, the bird flies off. One might reasonably ask whether this behavior is simply stimulus-bound. After all, there are behaviors like this in the animal

[9] *The Machinery of the Brain* (McGraw Hill, 1963), 82, quoted in Daniel Dennett, *Elbow Room: The Varieties of Free Will Worth Wanting* (MIT Press, 1984), 11.

[10] Carolyn Ristau, 'Aspects of the Cognitive Ethology of an Injury-Feigning Bird, the Piping Plover', in Carolyn Ristau (ed), *Cognitive Ethology: The Minds of Other Animals* (Lawrence Erlbaum Associates, 1991), 91–126.

world which are simply wired in, like the frog's tongue-flicking, and show no sign of sensitivity to other information which the animal may, in some sense, possess. But the piping plover's broken wing display is not like this. Thus, for example, if a human being walks on a path which would come close to the nest, the plover will approach the individual and perform the broken wing display. But if that person continues on her path without disturbing the nest, and follows this same path on a daily basis, then the plover will stop performing the display. When a different individual approaches, however, on the very same path, the plover goes back to its broken wing performance. This is not some stimulus-bound behavior. In order to explain it, we need to see the plover as picking up information about its environment and integrating it with stored information about the past. Here we have something requiring more than mere S-R connections.

Finally, there are creatures still more sophisticated than piping plovers. These creatures have states which not only register information about the environment—like thermostats and paramecia—and not only have states which form part of a representational system which interacts in ways dependent on the content of those states—like piping plovers—but these creatures also have second-order states, ones which carry information about the states which carry information about the environment. These second-order states are informationally integrated with the first-order states to form a far more flexible and responsive representational system. Adult human beings are creatures of this sort.

Where should we draw the line separating individuals who do have beliefs from those who do not? Now most of us would agree that individuals of the first sort described above—plants, thermostats, and so on—have no beliefs. And it is equally clear that individuals of the third sort, adult human beings, do have beliefs. But where do those in the second category belong? Should they be counted among the believers, along with adult human beings, or are they merely individuals with information-bearing states—like plants and thermostats—but utterly lacking in beliefs? Common sense and a good deal of work in the science of cognitive ethology would have it that many non-human animals do have genuine beliefs.[11] Brandom, Davidson, Haugeland, McDowell, Sellars,

---

[11] I have reviewed the relevant literature in cognitive ethology in favor of this claim in *Knowledge and its Place in Nature* (Oxford University Press, 2002), ch. 2. See also Colin Allen

and Williams[12] disagree. This is not merely a terminological dispute. It is, instead, a dispute about fundamental issues of both epistemology and metaphysics.

What is at stake here? According to Williams, 'The fundamental issue is whether being a believer requires a measure of rational self-awareness: the capacity to assess beliefs for their epistemic credentials.'[13] As we have seen, having beliefs is more than just a matter of having information-bearing states. After all, a thermostat, and even a piece of litmus paper, have information-bearing states. In order for an information-bearing state to qualify as a belief, according to Williams et al., it must be sensitive to reasons. The color of the litmus paper, for example, is sensitive to features of the external environment, but this is not enough, surely, to constitute a sensitivity to reasons. As Williams explains,

What we [Williams, Davidson, and Brandom[14]] argue, in our different ways, is that sensitivity to reasons or epistemic responsibility requires the *capacity* for assessing the credibility of one's commitments, revising them if need be. This capacity requires extensive knowledge of one's epistemic strengths and weaknesses: for example, the sorts of things one is or is not good at recognizing.[15]

Sensitivity to reasons, then, is a matter of epistemic responsibility which, in turn, requires a capacity for certain sorts of self-knowledge. Thus, on this view, it is impossible to reason or even have beliefs unless one also has second-order beliefs; it is impossible to have knowledge without also having second-order knowledge.

Now one might think that a natural view to hold about many non-human animals is that they have first-order beliefs—beliefs about their environment—but that they have no second-order beliefs at all. Many non-human animals, and young children, are thus believers; they are cognitive beings, even though they are incapable of having second-order

---

and Marc Bekoff, *Species of Mind: The Philosophy and Biology of Cognitive Ethology* (MIT Press, 1997).

[12] In *Knowledge and its Place in Nature*, I described Williams's view as one according to which non-human animals do have beliefs, but do not have knowledge. It is now entirely clear that this is not Williams's view: he rejects the claim that non-human animals have beliefs. See 'Is Knowledge a Natural Phenomenon?'.

[13] 'Is Knowledge a Natural Phenomenon?', 201.

[14] Williams is explicitly discussing these authors in the quoted passage. But the remarks he makes apply equally, it may be argued, to Haugeland, McDowell, and Sellars as well.

[15] 'Is Knowledge a Natural Phenomenon?', 208.

beliefs. This is the view I favor. But if Williams *et al.* are correct, the class of beings who have first-order beliefs and yet are utterly lacking in second-order beliefs is, of necessity, empty. It is only possible to have first-order beliefs if one also engages in a substantial amount of self-scrutiny, evaluating one's own cognitive position. One certainly needn't evaluate the epistemic credentials of every belief one holds; absolutely no one does this, and, indeed, no one could. But one simply doesn't count as a cognitive being—a creature with beliefs and other propositional attitudes—unless one does, at least at times, engage in a certain amount of self-scrutiny. Without such self-scrutiny, one does not count as forming beliefs; one is merely, like the piece of litmus paper, registering information. This kind of self-scrutiny, however, requires beliefs about one's own beliefs. If one is to take responsibility for one's beliefs, one must direct one's attention to them and, at least at times, consider the possibility that one might be wrong. This, of course, requires forming beliefs about one's beliefs. One thus cannot even have first-order beliefs unless one has second-order beliefs as well. Thus, anyone who argues that non-human animals or young children lack second-order beliefs, thereby succeeds, as Williams would have it, in making the case that such animals lack beliefs of any kind. On this view, then, there are individuals with informational states but no beliefs; and there are creatures with both first-order as well as second-order beliefs; but there simply could not be any creatures with first-order beliefs but no second-order beliefs at all. Second-order belief is a prerequisite for believing on the basis of reasons, and believing on the basis of reasons is a prerequisite for belief itself.

One last point. On this view, unlike Shoemaker's account, it is not the case that each individual instance of reasoning need be accompanied by a higher-order belief which licenses the inference. Instead, periodic acts of self-scrutiny are sufficient to satisfy the requirement of epistemic responsibility. This weakening of Shoemaker's requirement thereby avoids the infinite regress.[16]

---

[16] One might still wonder, even if the regress is thereby avoided, how well motivated the resulting account turns out to be. Thus, one might find it perfectly plausible to suggest that, so long as first-order belief acquisition is periodically assessed by way of some sort of higher-order monitoring, one's first-order beliefs are thereby shown to be epistemically responsible. But if this is the way one thinks about epistemic responsibility, the regress will not be avoided. For now in order to arrive at one's second-order beliefs in a responsible way, one will have to, at least periodically, monitor them by way of still higher-order assessment. And so on. The

2.4 Is it possible to have first-order beliefs without also having higher-order beliefs?

How do things look from the other side? Let us return to our three categories of individuals, representative members of which included plants, plovers, and people. As I see it, the striking difference between the first and the second category is this: while the first category includes individuals with information-bearing states, the states in these individuals do not add up to a representational system; in the second category, however, the information-bearing states do constitute such a system. As has been pointed out, it is not only plants which have information-bearing states; such states are also possessed by thermostats and even pieces of litmus paper. The fact that an individual has information-bearing states, by itself, does not show that the individual has any sort of psychology at all. When we move, however, from organisms with states which bear information about the environment to those with states which form a representational system, we thereby make the transition to creatures with propositional attitudes. As I see it, these are creatures with full-blown beliefs, desires, and so on; these are genuine cognitive beings.

When we look at the plover's sophisticated behavior, we see not only that it registers information about its environment, but these internal information-bearing states interact with one another to allow for more sensitive interactions with the environment. The plover first registers information about a potential threat—the human beings walking toward the nest—and takes appropriate action by engaging in the broken wing display. When the plover discovers, after repeated interactions with this particular individual, that no threat is present, she ceases to respond by engaging in the display. This requires the integration of new information with old, and this is why we need to posit a representational system to account for such sophisticated behavior. But, as I see it, there is now every reason to regard these informational interactions as cases of reasoning: they are, after all, transitions involving the interaction among representational states on the basis of their content.

Consider a second case of sophisticated non-human behavior, the case of tool use in apes. Here is Richard Byrne's description of a famous such case:

---

regress would then return. I will not pursue this issue further. Certainly this view does not generate a regress in the very direct way which Shoemaker's view does.

The wild chimpanzee is 'presented' with a termite mound, initially with no hole, in the African bush. (To be precise, only a few dozen rather inconspicuous termite nests are located in the home range of 15–20 square kilometers of forest and bush. A random day's walk would miss all of them.) The range of objects with which a mound might be probed (or prodded, or struck) is huge; very few of these natural objects are tried. Even the hole has to be made, and this can only be done in certain parts of the mound where termites are getting ready to emerge, at a certain time of year . . . The edible termites are not visible at all. Probing must be done delicately, and often the other hand is used as a guide and support. Hasty poking destroys the tool; hasty pulling out dislodges any attached termites. There is, in short, a lot to learn: termite fishing is a sophisticated skill.[17]

The chimpanzee, it seems to me, understands what it is doing. The sophistication of the behavior, the way in which the various subtle details of termite fishing are learned, the way in which the chimpanzee is responsive to success and failure of prior attempts, all tell in favor of viewing this behavior as involving significant cognitive achievements. Williams *et al.* frequently emphasize the connection between having beliefs and understanding, and I agree that there is such a connection. Plants, thermostats, and pieces of litmus paper have no understanding of their environment. But it is clear from the above description that chimpanzees do have such understanding. While they may be utterly lacking in an understanding of their own mental states, such a lack of understanding does not in any way preclude an understanding of the external environment.

I also want to agree with Williams *et al.* that having beliefs requires a sensitivity to reasons, and I believe that the behavior of the plovers and the chimpanzees shows that they are sensitive to reason. When the plover encounters a reason to stop engaging in the broken wing display, it stops; when the chimpanzee encounters a reason to modify its method of fishing for termites, it responds appropriately. As I see it, meta-cognitive evaluation is only one way to show a sensitivity to reasons. Just as constant self-monitoring is unnecessary for such sensitivity, self-monitoring of any sort is unnecessary. This is not to say that one might not achieve a greater degree of sensitivity by way of meta-cognitive monitoring. But, at the same time, one should not simply assume that greater reliability is

---

[17] 'Social and Technical Forms of Primate Intelligence', in F. de Waal (ed.), *Tree of Origin: What Primate Behavior Can Tell Us about Human Social Evolution* (Harvard University Press, 2001), 163.

inevitably the product of some such self-scrutiny, as we saw above in section 1.3. Once one sees that meta-cognitive evaluation may sometimes result in less sensitivity to reason, sometimes result in no change in one's sensitivity to reason, and sometimes result in greater sensitivity to reason, one is faced with a choice: does one care about such self-scrutiny regardless of its efficacy in improving reliability, or does one care about it only insofar as it is instrumental in producing a greater sensitivity to reason? I don't think that the first of these two options is reasonable. But the second option makes reliability fundamental, and views meta-cognition as one process among many which may, in some cases, aid in generating a responsiveness to reasons.

Consider how we are to tell the story of cognitive development in children, that is, creatures who make the transition from the second of our categories to the third. As developmental psychologists tell us,[18] mental state concepts are fairly late arrivals on the conceptual scene: children do not have beliefs about beliefs, for example, until roughly the age of 4 and a half. Now one way to tell the story of cognitive development, indeed, the way most developmental psychologists tell the story, is that, early on, children have a robust set of beliefs about their physical environment; it is only quite a bit later that they come to have beliefs about mental states. If such an account is correct, as I believe it to be, then we may give the obvious account of the sophisticated behaviors of 3 year olds, namely, that they have an extensive set of beliefs about their environment, and elaborate desires as well, and these beliefs and desires jointly conspire to produce behavior. Children under the age of 4 learn a great deal about their environment, and the natural account of this learning requires that they be seen as engaging in reasoning: new information is not simply registered; it is combined with pre-existing belief to produce new belief. If we see things in this way, as I would suggest we should, then children under the age of 4 will be regarded as having propositional attitudes, but they will not be seen, from the beginning, as having second-order propositional attitudes. The various concepts of the propositional attitudes themselves—the concepts of belief and desire, for example—are far more complex than the concepts acquired early on. Needless to say, the concepts of truth and

---

[18] See e.g. Astington, *Child's Discovery of the Mind*; Alison Gopnik and Andrew Meltzoff, *Words, Thoughts and Theories* (MIT Press, 1997); Janet Astington *et al.* (eds), *Developing Theories of Mind* (Cambridge University Press, 1988).

falsity are extraordinarily sophisticated; it should be no surprise that various physical object concepts are acquired long before there is any understanding of the idea of truth.

If we insist, however, that it is impossible to have first-order beliefs unless one also has second-order beliefs, then the developmental story becomes far more difficult to tell. One will need an explanation of the kinds of learning which occur before the age of 4 which does not in any way appeal to beliefs or desires. On this account, if we acknowledge that children do not acquire the concept of belief until age 4, we will need to insist that there are no beliefs of any kind before that age, and no desires, presumably, as well. At the same time, it must be recognized that these children are not simple S-R individuals; they are far more sophisticated than plants and thermostats. One may, of course, insist that the term 'belief' is an honorific which is to be reserved only for creatures who have second-order beliefs as well as first-order states, but the motivation for this kind of insistence is beginning to look strained. The explanation of early behavior would now require 'proto-beliefs' and 'proto-desires'. Only when these states themselves become mentally represented, as part of the very same representational system, do they attain the status of genuine beliefs and desires. There seems to be nothing in the phenomena themselves which would justify such a terminological distinction. More than this, one is forced to tell a story about concept acquisition which is extremely implausible: instead of supposing that physical object concepts are acquired early on and that mental state concepts are later arrivals, as the standard story would have it, Williams et al. are forced to say that there are no physical object concepts prior to the acquisition of mental state concepts. It is hard to make sense of such an account of cognitive development.

Note, in particular, that the standard proposed by Williams et al.—no beliefs without meta-beliefs—is far more demanding than the suggestion that there are no beliefs without language.[19] Children not only have a very

---

[19] Similar difficulties face José Bermudez, as I point out in my response to his critical remarks on *Knowledge and its Place and Nature*. See Bermudez, 'Knowledge, Naturalism and Cognitive Ethology: Kornblith's *Knowledge and its Place in Nature*', *Philosophical Studies*, 127 (2006), 317–35; Kornblith, 'Reply to Bermudez and BonJour', *Philosophical Studies*, 127 (2006), 337–49. Bermudez develops his view at length in *Thinking without Words* (Oxford University Press, 2003).

substantial vocabulary at age 3; they are speaking in complicated sentences. Thus, Steven Pinker remarks:

Between the late 2s and mid-3s, children's language blooms into fluent gram-matical conversation so rapidly that it overwhelms the researchers who study it; no one has worked out the exact sequence. Sentence length increases steadily and, because grammar is a combinatorial system, the number of syntactic types increases exponentially, doubling every month, reaching the thousands before the third birthday.[20]

Thus, if we follow Williams, then it is not just piping plovers and chim-panzees who will be resigned to the realm of non-believers; it is children below the age of 4 as well, in spite of the fact that many of them are fluent language users. This is, to say the least, hard to credit. Davidson is no better off. While he is well-known for his view that there are no beliefs without language, this is not to say that he thinks language use is sufficient for belief. Indeed, what he suggests is that one cannot have beliefs unless one has 'the idea of an objective, public truth'.[21] It is safe to say that such a concept is not possessed by 4 year olds. Haugeland requires that genuine believers have a capacity for what he calls 'existential commitment',[22] a kind of commitment of which young children and animals are clearly incapable.[23] Brandom, McDowell, and Sellars are no better off in this respect. Thus, in all of these authors, the standard account of cognitive development must be rejected in favor of an account which sees proto-beliefs giving way to beliefs only when some critical juncture—the acqui-sition of second-order beliefs, the acquisition of the concept of truth, the capacity for existential commitment—is reached. Any such account of cognitive development is terribly implausible. And this, of course, reflects

---

[20] 'Language Acquisition', in Lila Gleitman and Mark Liberman (eds), *An Invitation to Cognitive Science*, i, 2nd edn. (MIT Press, 1995), 143–4.

[21] 'Thought and Talk', 170.

[22] He thus remarks: 'It is the capacity for this sort of commitment that I am inclined to think is relatively recent–almost certainly more recent than language, and perhaps more recent than cities and writing. Like city-building and writing, the possibility of existential commitment is part of a cultural heritage (not just a biological or "natural" capacity).' *Having Thought: Essays in the Metaphysics of Mind*, 2.

[23] Haugeland makes this point quite clear: 'there are senses in which many animals can be said to "know", "want", and even "understand" things around them; but these are not the same as the senses in which people can be said to know, want, and understand things. Classing these uncritically together is as great an obstacle to insight as was classing whales with fish or the sun with the planets.' Ibid.

badly on the suggestion that we cannot have first-order belief, or sensitivity to reasons, without higher-order belief.

McDowell seems to recognize that there is a problem here.

Now it is not even clearly intelligible to suppose a creature might be born at home in the space of reasons. Human beings are not: they are born mere animals, and they are transformed into thinkers and intentional agents in the course of coming to maturity. This transformation risks looking mysterious.[24]

So what is McDowell's solution to this problem? If we insist that young children do not have beliefs and are not sensitive to reasons, how exactly do we account for the ever-increasing cognitive sophistication which we see during this period of pre-belief? And how do children make the transition from being creatures utterly lacking in beliefs and insensitive to reason to being creatures who do have beliefs and are sensitive to reason? Here is what McDowell says:

A mere animal, moved only by the sorts of things that move mere animals and exploiting the sorts of contrivances that are open to mere animals, could not single-handedly emancipate itself into possession of understanding. Human beings mature into being at home in the space of reasons or, what comes to the same thing, living their lives in the world; we can make sense of that by noting that the language into which a human being is first initiated stands over against her as a prior embodiment of mindedness, of the possibility of an orientation to the world.[25]

So it is language learning, according to McDowell, that allows for this transition. Now there are a number of problems with this. First, as I just noted, children learn a language prior to having the very concepts which McDowell and others see as a prerequisite for having beliefs. So the suggestion that language learning somehow ushers the child into the space of reasons seems to give the child beliefs just a bit too soon. Second, and more importantly, this suggestion seems to ignore, rather than address, the very real problem of accounting for all of the learning which goes on prior to the alleged acquisition of beliefs. And finally, the suggestion seems to be a failure even on its own terms. Even if we suppose, with McDowell, that there are no beliefs prior to language acquisition, and that the child is initiated into the space of reasons in the very acquisition of language, we have merely relocated the problem rather than solved it: what was once a problem for the individual child now becomes a problem for the origin

---

[24] *Mind and World*, 125.   [25] Ibid.

of language itself. If children are only able to acquire intentional states because they are raised in an environment in which they can be initiated into language, exactly how did the first languages come about, since, as McDowell would have it, there were no beliefs prior to the existence of language, but one cannot make the transition from being a creature without beliefs to being a creature with them without being embedded in a culture where language is spoken? If children can acquire beliefs only because they are enculturated by way of a 'prior embodiment of mind-edness', then we seem to be committed to the existence of that prior embodiment all the way back in time. This is a rather high price to pay for insisting that children do not have beliefs until they are conceptually quite sophisticated.

Any suggestion that we are forced somehow to make sense of this by the fact that animal information processing is nothing but the operation of causal mechanisms, and *therefore* cannot involve either reason responsiveness or belief,[26] surely runs afoul of the problem that it proves too much. Adult human belief acquisition is causally mediated; the science of psychology explains it, just as much as the information processing in children and non-human animals, by bringing it under the scope of psychological law. If this is sufficient to undermine the attribution of belief and sensitivity to reasons, then no one has beliefs at all. This may be congenial to eliminitivists, but it was not where this argument was supposed to lead.

2.5 Are philosophers and psychologists talking past one another?

I have been arguing that the standard account of belief which we find in developmental psychologists runs contrary to the suggestions of Brandom, Davidson, Haugeland, McDowell, Sellars, and Williams, and that these philosophers offer us an account of belief which will make it difficult to tell a plausible story about cognitive development. But perhaps this kind of argument begs the question against these authors by presupposing a claim they would all reject: that belief is a natural kind. I have, after all, supposed that there is a certain natural phenomenon, believing, which occurs in

---

[26] Precisely this sort of move is strongly suggested by the emphasis on the importance of the contrast between 'the space of causes' and 'the space of reasons'.

human adults, and I have been asking whether this very same phenomenon occurs in non-humans and young children. I have assumed, as a working hypothesis, that there is indeed a unified phenomenon of believing, and that it is possible to give an account of it which explains the causal role which beliefs play in producing behavior. Developmental psychologists in fact offer just such a unified explanatory account, and those who set significantly higher standards for belief thereby offer a view of this phenomenon which stands in the way of a plausible unified account. To my mind, this counts in favor of the view of the developmentalists, and against the views of Williams *et al.*

But perhaps this is unfair. Haugeland explicitly rejects the view that the propositional attitudes constitute a natural kind. He says that they are 'part of a cultural heritage (not just a biological or "natural" capacity)'.[27] And Williams says that 'knowledge is not a natural phenomenon';[28] he makes quite clear that he has the same view of belief, and that he sees this view in Brandom and Davidson as well. So if these philosophers reject the view that belief is a natural kind, that the notion of belief they are trying to articulate must therefore fit in to some well-confirmed scientific theory which explains the causal role which beliefs play in producing behavior, then one might reasonably think it unfair to argue against their views by pointing out that they fail to fit in with any such account.

Let me therefore acknowledge that these philosophers are not trying to offer a scientific account of belief, or even an account of belief which is compatible with the best available scientific theories. Even if there is a natural kind of which the developmental psychologists are giving a well-confirmed account, that natural kind is not the object of study which Williams *et al.* are talking about. They are talking about something else.

So what is it that these philosophers mean to be talking about, if it is not the natural phenomenon which developmental psychologists study? Merely rejecting the view that belief is a natural kind does not, of course, relieve one of the responsibility to locate the subject of one's investigation. These philosophers attempt to offer an account of the nature of belief; they merely deny that belief, as they understand it, is an object of scientific study.

---

[27] *Having Thought*, 2.   [28] 'Is Knowledge a Natural Phenomenon?', 194.

Thus, for example, if a marine biologist attempts to explain what sponges are, and someone who is interested in household products should come along and insist that he too is interested in sponges, but not the natural kind that goes by that name, I think none of us would have any trouble understanding what is being claimed. There is a natural kind which marine biologists refer to with the word 'sponge'. There is a household cleaning product which is also referred to as a 'sponge'. These are two different things, and there is no need for the theory of the household product to answer to the science of marine biology. Household sponges are not a natural kind, one might reasonably say. The word 'sponge' is simply ambiguous.

So unless these philosophers wish to reject the scientific account of belief which is embedded in current work in developmental psychology—and none of them attempt to engage with that literature—then we should assume that they view any such account as no more relevant to what they are doing than the marine biological account of sponges is to the investigation of household products. The latter investigation may have an integrity of its own without taking on the (irrelevant) work of marine biologists.

If this is the right way to see those who reject the view that belief and knowledge are natural kinds, then some case needs to be made that there is, as in the case of sponges, a genuine ambiguity in our talk of beliefs, with a non-scientific notion sitting side by side with the scientific one. And we need to have some sense, as we clearly do in the case of sponges, of what the phenomenon is which the philosophical account is supposed to answer to.

In the case of belief, however, this task is complicated by the fact that the non-scientific notion of belief which these philosophers mean to explicate seems to be called on to explain many of the very same phenomena which the scientific notion addresses. Thus, all of the philosophers under discussion view beliefs as causes of behavior. In addition, explanations are sometimes offered which seem to be presented as rivals to the scientific account. For example, Michael Williams defends the implication of his account that non-human animals do not have beliefs by attempting to locate an important difference between human and non-human mental representations:

We might say, animals don't need the capacity for epistemic assessment because they don't test hypotheses: they test themselves. But this is why they are not truly

sensitive to reasons. They cannot really change their minds, though the information-acquiring and processing capacities of the species can change over time.[29]

This kind of argument puzzles me. Williams seems to be arguing that there
is an important difference between human belief and the mental representations of non-human animals, and because they are different in this
fundamental way, they should not be seen as belonging to the same kind.
While I am certainly sympathetic in principle with this sort of argument,
this sounds like an argument that animal mental representations and
human beliefs constitute different natural kinds; it doesn't sound at all
like an argument for the view that human belief doesn't constitute a
natural kind at all.

But this is not the only problem with Williams's argument, for the claim
he makes about the difference between human and non-human animals is
also untrue. Williams presents a picture of non-human animals as acquiring
information about their environment by way of processes which are hard-
wired and thus insensitive to new information. According to Williams,
'the information-acquiring and processing capacities of the species can
change over time' in the case of non-human animals, but, unlike humans,
they do not change within the life of an individual. This is certainly the
case with the frog's hard-wired response to flies and BBs. It might change
in the species in response to evolutionary pressures, if, for example, frogs
were to find themselves in an environment where moving BBs are
plentiful, but this process of information acquisition is not going to change
in the life of a single frog; it does not respond to new information the frog
comes to possess. The same is true of *Sphex*'s highly routinized behavior in
preparing its burrow for its newly laid eggs. Williams's claim about the
difference between human and animal cognition amounts to the suggestion that all animal cognition is like this.

We need not look to work with primates to see that this is not remotely
true. Skinner's early work with rats and pigeons[30] shows that they are
responsive to changes in their environment, and that they easily learn how
to go about attaining a variety of rewards, displaying a subtle sensitivity to
the ways in which their environment has changed. The mechanisms of
learning in animals are complex and varied, as even the most conservative

[29]   Ibid. 209.
[30]   B. F. Skinner and Charles Ferster, *Schedules of Reinforcement* (Appleton Century Crofts,
1957).

writers on this topic allow.[31] The simple reflexes we see in the case of the frog and the wasp are not the rule in animal information processing; they are not even the rule in frogs[32] or wasps.[33] Even in the case of fairly stereotyped behaviors—such as the broken-wing display in piping plovers, used to mislead would-be predators—new information may often be integrated with old in ways completely unlike the hard-wired fly-swallowing behavior of frogs and the striking perseverance of *Sphex*. And as we see in the example of termite fishing in apes, animals are capable of extraordinarily complicated feats of learning. The fact of animal learning has been well-documented for as long as there has been serious work on animal behavior. Animal learning requires the integration of new information with old, and this, in turn, makes itself manifest in the ways in which still later information is processed. All of this is quite prosaic. More interesting, and far more complex, are the phenomena of problem-solving and innovation.[34] But we need not examine such subtle phenomena in order to see that the manner in which animals process information may change over time.

Williams's suggestion that non-human animals 'don't test hypotheses: they test themselves' is very much in the spirit of Quine's famous suggestion that 'creatures inveterately wrong in their inductions have a pathetic but praiseworthy tendency to die before reproducing their kind'.[35] Williams sees the tendency of animals to die if their inferences are inaccurate, however, as the only means by which their inferential accuracy may be improved. This presents us with an extremely impoverished view of animal learning, and a view thoroughly at odds with the facts. The suggestion that non-human animals do not have beliefs cannot be justified in this way.

Williams *et al.* need to provide some other reason for thinking that the kind of belief of which they are giving an account is both different from the one which psychologists are examining and legitimate in its own right.

---

[31] For one conservative survey, see Sara Shettleworth, *Cognition, Evolution and Behavior* (Oxford University Press, 1998), 95–232.

[32] See e.g. Darcy Kelley, 'Vocal Communication in Frogs', *Current Opinion in Neurobiology*, 14 (2004), 751–7.

[33] H. E. Evans, *The Comparative Ethology of the Sand Wasps* (Harvard University Press, 1966).

[34] See e.g. Simon Reader and Kevin Laland (eds), *Animal Innovation* (Oxford University Press, 2003).

[35] 'Natural Kinds', in *Ontological Relativity and Other Essays* (Columbia University Press, 1969), 126.

They offer a number of additional reasons for thinking that knowledge and belief are not natural kinds, that is, that the kind of belief in which they are interested is different from the one which psychologists investigate. Let us turn to examine those reasons.

2.6 Is there a social dimension to the propositional attitudes?

When Haugeland addresses this issue, he contrasts the idea that propositional attitudes are biological or natural kinds with the suggestion that they are 'part of a cultural heritage'.[36] Williams too brings up the issue of a social dimension to propositional attitudes in this context.

Consideration of the demands of epistemic responsibility helps to clarify the ways in which knowledge is and is not a social undertaking. To become sensitive to reasons is to learn what can and cannot reasonably be questioned, and why. Thus acquiring sensitivity to reasons requires a lot of know-how, as well as extensive meta-knowledge. To become a knower is to become acculturated. This is not something that one could, even in principle, do for oneself.[37]

Brandom and Davidson, each in their own way, also argue that there are certain social dimensions to the propositional attitudes. These suggestions raise two different questions. First, are there important social dimensions to the propositional attitudes? And second, if the propositional attitudes do, in some sense, have a social dimension to them, does this thereby show that they do not constitute natural kinds? I will address each of these questions in turn.

Let us look at the quotation from Williams carefully. 'To be sensitive to reasons,' he tells us, 'is to learn what can and cannot reasonably be questioned, and why.' Much of human learning certainly involves learning 'what can and cannot reasonably be questioned', and much of this is straightforwardly social. As Williams remarks, acculturation involves this very sort of learning, and to learn what can and cannot reasonably be questioned certainly does allow one to become sensitive to reasons. So this sort of cultural process is one way in which one might become sensitive to reason. Talk of 'questioning' here may also suggest something typical of the human case, namely language use, something crucial, of course, in

---

[36] *Having Thought*, 2.   [37] 'Is Knowledge a Natural Phenomenon?', 208.

Davidson's account. But social learning, by itself, needn't involve language use. Chimpanzees learn how to fish for termites from their conspecifics, but the skill of termite fishing is not taught in a way which involves linguistic communication. One might emphasize social dimensions to learning without thereby committing oneself to any view at all about the essentiality of linguistic communication, even if such communication is, of course, the norm in human social learning.

Talk of 'what can . . . be questioned', however, while it certainly suggests something linguistic, and social as well, need not perhaps involve either of these features. I may, without any social interaction at all, question myself about what I ought to believe. And if all one means by coming 'to learn what can and cannot be reasonably questioned' is coming to learn how inquiry ought to proceed—which possibilities to take seriously and which one may reasonably ignore—then the linguistic dimension seems optional here as well. The chimpanzee, in learning to fish for termites, learns to take certain things for granted and to carefully check on others. And although the chimpanzee learns this particular skill socially, not everything learned is learned in this way. Interaction with the world is one good way to learn which things one may take for granted, and which things need to be checked. The world, after all, has a way of informing one if one fails to check on things which should not be taken for granted.

Now the kind of learning 'what can and cannot reasonably be questioned' which is essential for having a sensitivity to reasons is surely the kind involved in coming to learn how inquiry ought to proceed. But it is now clear that, even if this learning is typically both social and linguistic in the human case, such learning requires neither social nor linguistic contributions. Given sufficiently flexible native capacities, interaction with the world may teach one how to proceed with one's inquiries by teaching one what one should test and what one may simply rely upon. Creatures who have such sophisticated capacities, whether they have second-order beliefs or not, whether they have linguistic capacities or not, and whether their learning is social or not, thereby display a sensitivity to reasons. The suggestion that a sensitivity to reasons is essentially social, or cultural, is thus simply mistaken.

But let us suppose, just for the sake of argument, that sensitivity to reasons is essentially social or cultural. Why should one think, as Williams and Haugeland clearly do, that this would show that belief and knowledge are not natural kinds? Why should we think that 'social' and 'natural' are contraries? Here is what Williams says on this score, in explaining why he is opposed to the idea that epistemology should be naturalized:

> to claim that knowledge need not be naturalized does not mean that it should be understood in some 'anti-naturalist' (let alone supernaturalist) way. It is to claim, rather, that although we can illuminate the concept of knowledge, and explain why it matters to us to have a concept like that, knowledge is not a proper object of theory, scientific or otherwise.[38]

So epistemology, on Williams's conception, will 'illuminate the concept of knowledge', and 'explain why it matters to us to have a concept like that', but, at the same time, we should think that 'knowledge is not a proper object of theory'. What does this mean?

Consider, by way of contrast, the concept of disease. Historians of medicine might attempt to illuminate the concept of disease and explain how it has changed over time. They might, in addition, explain why it matters to us to have a concept like that. But in this case, of course, we do have a proper object of scientific theorizing, and it is precisely by way of successful scientific theorizing about the nature of disease that we may shed light on why it is so important for us to have a concept of such a thing. It is only by understanding what diseases really are that we may understand why it is important for us to have a concept of them. So in this case, the kinds of conceptual investigations which Williams favors in the case of knowledge simply are not at odds with the kind of naturalistic investigation I endorse. But in the case of disease, although the concept is, in some sense, socially constructed, and our knowledge of diseases is socially mediated, disease itself is not a social kind, and it is for this reason, no doubt, that Williams would see the case of disease as different in kind from the case of knowledge.

So let us look at an example of a social kind. Consider the case of 'democratically elected government'. This is a kind which is social through and through if anything is. Here we may certainly attempt to illuminate the concept of a democratically elected government, trying to say just what this kind of government comes to; and we may attempt to say something about why it is important that we have a concept of this kind. But here too, it seems, we may theorize about democratically

---

[38] Ibid. 209.

elected governments themselves, and attempt to discover what the connection is, if any, between this form of government and other social conditions. Indeed, this very form of theorizing is familiar in the social sciences. The fact that this is a socially constructed kind does not in any way make it an improper object of theorizing. Social kinds may, after all, have a degree of stability that allows for significant causal explanations in terms of them.[39] Indeed, it is for this very reason that social theories may be so illuminating. If social kinds were not an object of proper theorizing, then the very idea of social science would be a sham. I take it that Williams is not endorsing the radical claim that there is no such thing as a legitimate social science.

But why then should we think that there is some essential conflict between the alleged social character of knowledge, or our concept of knowledge, and regarding knowledge as a proper object of theory? The social dimension of knowledge is important for Williams, I believe, not simply qua social, but rather because, on his view, it provides the grounding for normativity. In the end, it is not that the social and the natural are seen as automatically opposed by Williams, but rather that the normative and the natural are seen as antithetical. Thus, in summarizing Brandom's view on the nature of reasons, a view with which he has a good deal of sympathy, Williams remarks:

we cannot capture content-determining inferential relations without recourse to *normative* vocabulary. Reasons must be intelligible as *good* reasons. Moreover, those to whom we attribute sensitivity to reasons must be such that we can see them as taking *normative attitudes*—treating some reasons as good, others as not so good—for this is what, in practical terms, sensitivity to reasons comes to.[40]

As a number of philosophers now put it, what is at issue here is whether there is a fundamental split between the 'space of reasons' and the 'space of causes'.

We can agree with Williams (and Brandom) that sensitivity to reasons requires 'treating some reasons as good, others as not so good'. It is one thing, however, to show a sensitivity to reasons, quite another to conceptualize

---

[39] This point is nicely developed in Ron Mallon's 'Social Roles, Social Construction and Stability', in Frederick F. Schmitt (ed.), *Socializing Metaphysics: The Nature of Social Reality* (Rowman & Littlefield, 2003).

[40] 'Is Knowledge a Natural Phenomenon?', 201.

reasons *as* reasons.[41] As we have seen in our earlier discussion of second-order belief, sensitivity to reasons may be achieved even without having the concept of a reason, or of a belief. If all Williams means by his talk of 'normative attitudes' is the differential treatment of reasons—treating some as good and others as not so good—then normative attitudes are had by non-human animals, and they are not the exclusive property of human beings. If, on the other hand, talk of normative attitudes is meant to be more demanding, requiring the possession of normative concepts, then we have been given no reason at all to think that sensitivity to reasons requires having attitudes of this kind.

Wherever we stand, however, on the question about what a sensitivity to reasons requires, we have been given no reason at all to think that normative features of belief and knowledge cannot be objects of theory. Work in cognitive ethology and human cognitive psychology deals with the very sensitivities to which Williams directs our attention. There is important theoretical work being done on the nature of concepts, and how it is that concepts play a role in cognition. Whether these concepts be social or not, whether they be normative or not, has proven simply irrelevant to productive theorizing. In the face of these successful programs of research, it simply will not do to insist that knowledge cannot be an object of theory.

The attempt to provide an account of reasons, belief, and knowledge as objects of philosophical theorizing which somehow distinguishes them from the phenomena which psychologists seek to investigate thereby fails. There is no distinctively philosophical concept of belief which is both different from the object of scientific investigation and, at the same time, legitimate in its own right. The additional higher-order requirements with which Williams *et al.* seek to burden belief are thus shown to be untenable.

2.7 Conclusion

When we reason, beliefs are brought about by other beliefs. It is clear, however, that not every case of one belief being brought about by another involves reasoning. We are thus led to ask just what else might be required

---

[41] Thus, note e.g. that someone may show a tremendous sensitivity to ragweed without conceptualizing ragweed *as* ragweed.

for reasoning to take place. One obvious suggestion involves an appeal to reflection: reasoning involves a higher-order belief about the transition from one belief to another; it is only when the transition from one belief to another takes place under the aegis of such a higher-order belief that we may legitimately speak of reasoning. The problem with such a simple requirement, of course, is that it leads immediately to an infinite regress.

Shoemaker has a tempting way to avoid the regress, or rather, to tame it. The regress only seems threatening if we think of the higher-order belief that one believes that *p* as metaphysically distinct from the first-order belief that *p*. Shoemaker argues, however, that these beliefs are not wholly distinct. To a first approximation, Shoemaker argues that higher-order belief supervenes on first-order belief. On such a view, we get higher-order beliefs for free, as it were. The regress, on such a view, is innocent.

As we have seen, however, such a view is implausible. As Shoemaker points out, higher-order beliefs aren't, strictly speaking, supervenient on first-order belief alone. They are, as he argues, supervenient on first-order belief plus rationality and a sufficient degree of conceptual sophistication. Once we see the importance of these other ingredients, however, it becomes clear that the relationship between them and higher-order belief is not merely constitutive, as Shoemaker would have it, but causal. This means that higher-order belief does not just tag along with first-order belief for free, however, and the attempt to domesticate the regress is thereby undermined.

A different kind of attempt to implicate reflection and higher-order belief in reasoning is found in the work of Brandom, Davidson, Haugeland, McDowell, Sellars, and Williams. As they see it, reasoning involves a sensitivity to reasons, and this requires epistemic responsibility. Epistemic responsibility, in turn, requires some sort of at least periodic higher-order monitoring of one's beliefs. Indeed, as these authors argue, such higher-order monitoring is a prerequisite for having beliefs at all.

Even leaving aside worries about the infinite regress, this view faces very substantial difficulties. It offers an account of belief which flies in the face of our best developmental theories, and it makes a mystery of the transition from the pre-belief stage of young children, as these authors see it, to fully fledged adult cognition. Any attempt to insist that when these philosophers talk about reasoning, belief, and knowledge, they are talking about something different than what psychologists discuss when they use the very same terms has been shown to be implausible. These philosophers cannot then simply duck the empirical consequences of their view.

Reasoning does, of course, require a sensitivity to reasons, and such a sensitivity may, at times, be achieved or even heightened, by way of thinking about reasons qua reasons. It may thus, at times, involve reflection and second-order belief. But higher-order belief is not a prerequisite for sensitivity to reasons. We may reason without forming beliefs about our beliefs, and without reflecting on the activity of reasoning. Second-order belief is not the special ingredient that makes reasoning possible. When we form higher-order beliefs, these are just additional cognitive elements that interact in predictable ways with the rest of our cognitive economy. Higher-order beliefs do not play a pre-eminent role in these interactions.

3

Freedom

Adult human beings are intellectually more sophisticated than other animals. Even if we allow, as I've argued we should, that many other animals have beliefs and desires, there is reason to believe that we may be the only species with second-order beliefs and desires. And this makes us far more complex intellectually than other animals.

My dog is moved by his beliefs and desires. When he hears food being poured into his dish in the kitchen, he comes running. He believes that there is food in his dish, and that is just what he wants. So his behavior is produced by a rational interaction of his beliefs and desires. And in that respect, he's just like me. My behavior too is, at times, produced by the rational interaction of my beliefs and desires.

But my dog, it is safe to say, never stops to consider whether he should believe the things he does. He doesn't stop to think, 'I wonder if I really have good evidence that there's food in my bowl.' He doesn't stop to consider whether he should want the things that he in fact wants, and he doesn't ever stop to consider whether he should do the things that he in fact does. He never stops to ask himself whether he is being the sort of dog he wants to be. He isn't conceptually sophisticated enough to have any of these thoughts. And the result of this is that he never stops to critically assess his beliefs, his desires, his motivations, his actions, or his character. And this is a respect in which he and I are different. I, like other adult human beings, do, at times, stop to assess these things. At a minimum, that makes me a more complex creature than my dog, intellectually speaking.

Some writers believe that this sort of intellectual sophistication which adult human beings have amounts to something far more important than just a difference in degree. The ability to critically assess one's beliefs, desires, motivations, actions, and character is connected, on certain views, with issues about freedom and responsibility. Freedom requires, on certain views, the ability to critically assess one's actions. Dogs may have genuine propositional attitudes, but their inability to reflect on their first-order states, and their attendant inability to critically assess those states, assures, on certain views, that they lack a crucial prerequisite for freedom and responsibility.

In this chapter, we will examine views which make the ability to reflect on one's first-order psychological states a prerequisite for freedom, or a particularly important sort of freedom. In the course of discussing a number of issues about agency, we will also be led to discuss a particular sort of agency—epistemic agency—which many have argued is deeply connected to the issues we have addressed in the first two chapters.

3.1 The infinite regress

In his seminal article, 'Freedom of the Will and the Concept of a Person', Harry Frankfurt draws a distinction between freedom of action and freedom of the will.

According to one familiar philosophical tradition, being free is fundamentally a matter of doing what one wants to do. Now the notion of an agent who does what he wants to do is by no means an altogether clear one: both the doing and the wanting, and the appropriate relation between them as well, require elucidation. But although its focus needs to be sharpened and its formulation refined, I believe that this notion does capture at least part of what is implicit in the idea of an agent who *acts* freely. It misses entirely, however, the peculiar content of the quite different idea of an agent whose *will* is free.[1]

Frankfurt's account of freedom of the will is best understood by way of a comparison between genuine persons and creatures Frankfurt calls *wantons*:

The wanton addict cannot or does not care which of his conflicting first-order desires wins out. His lack of concern is not due to his inability to find a convincing basis for a preference. It is due either to his lack of the capacity for reflection or to his mindless indifference to the enterprise of evaluating his own desires and motives. There is only one issue in the struggle to which his first-order conflict may lead: whether the one or the other of his conflicting desires is the stronger. Since he is moved by both desires, he will not be altogether satisfied by what he does no matter which of them is effective. But it makes no difference *to him*

---

[1] 'Freedom of the Will and the Concept of a Person', repr. in *The Importance of What we Care about: Philosophical Essays* (Cambridge University Press, 1988), 19–20.

whether his craving or his aversion gets the upper hand. He has no stake in the conflict between them and so, unlike the unwilling addict, he can neither win nor lose the struggle in which he is engaged. When a *person* acts, the desire by which he is moved is either the will he wants or a will he wants to be without. When a *wanton* acts, it is neither.

. . . It is only because a person has volitions of the second order that he is capable both of enjoying and of lacking freedom of the will. The concept of a person is not only, then, the concept of a type of entity that has both first-order desires and volitions of the second order. It can also be construed as the concept of a type of entity for whom the freedom of its will may be a problem. This concept excludes all wantons, both infrahuman and human, since they fail to satisfy an essential condition for the enjoyment of freedom of the will.[2]

Non-human animals, since they lack both second-order desires and second-order volitions, lack freedom of the will, although they may frequently do as they want, and, in that sense, act freely. Adult human beings, however, who at least typically have both kinds of second-order states, are capable of freedom of the will as well as free action.

There is reason to think that this is an especially important distinction. Notice that we do not hold animals and young children responsible for their behavior, and we do not hold them responsible for their behavior, it seems, because they are not the kinds of individuals that could be responsible for their behavior. When my neighbor's dog runs loose in my garden and destroys the flowers, it is not the dog who is responsible, but my neighbor. The dog should have been trained better, or, failing that, penned up. The respect in which the dog is not responsible is not merely a legal issue. Rather, the dog is not morally responsible for its behavior. The same, of course, is true of young children. But now Frankfurt's account seems to give us a perspicuous bit of terminology for describing what it is that adult human beings typically have, and young children and non-human animals inevitably lack, which explains why it is that adults are typically responsible for their behavior and children and animals are not. Adults may have freedom of the will, while children and non-human animals cannot. Adults have the capacity to reflect on and critically assess their beliefs, desires, motives, characters, and actions; children and non-human animals do not. Freedom of the will, and the capacity to act in ways for which one is morally responsible, requires the ability to reflect on, and critically assess, one's first-order mental states.

[2] Ibid. 18–19.

Let us consider Frankfurt's wanton addict who has conflicting first-order desires. Let us suppose that our wanton has the desire for heroin, but also, since he is hungry, a desire for food. Unfortunately, he currently has neither food nor heroin, and he doesn't have enough money to buy them both. He thus has conflicting desires. Frankfurt says that, since he faces such a conflict, 'he will not be altogether satisfied by what he does no matter which of them is effective', and this is surely right. But this in no way distinguishes the wanton from a person who has conflicting first-order desires and resolutely acts on one of them. When one wants two things and can't have them both, one will, inevitably, find oneself not fully satisfied. Frankfurt says that in cases of conflict, the wanton 'has no stake in the conflict' between his desires, and so 'he can neither win nor lose the struggle in which he is engaged'. This contrasts, Frankfurt tells us, with the person who has formed a higher-order preference to act on one or another desire, or who forms a volition to act on one of his desires, for the person wins his struggle if and only if his action conforms to his higher-order volition. On Frankfurt's view, in order to have a stake in the struggle between two first-order desires, one must have a second-order preference to act on one of them rather than the other.

But surely, if one sees things this way, then the same will be true in cases where one has no conflict in one's first-order desires at all: that is, Frankfurt should hold that, even when one's first-order desire is unopposed, one has no stake in whether it is satisfied unless one also has a second-order desire that it should be effective in action. And this is, indeed, Frankfurt's view. Frankfurt remarks,

> The essential characteristic of the wanton is that he does not care about his will. His desires move him to do certain things, without its being true of him either that he wants to be moved by those desires or that he prefers to be moved by other desires. The class of wantons includes all nonhuman animals that have desires and all very young children. Perhaps it also includes some adult human beings as well. In any case, adult human beings may be more or less wanton; they may act wantonly, in response to first-order desires concerning which they have no volitions of the second-order, more or less frequently.[3]

So let us consider what an action which exhibits freedom of the will must look like on Frankfurt's view. Suppose Annie has a desire to go to Paris,

---

[3] Ibid. 16–17.

and she knows that by buying a ticket on Air France, she can get there. If she buys the ticket straightaway, without reflecting on her first-order desire, then she acts wantonly. She is, in acting this way, acting freely, but she does not display freedom of the will. In particular, she acts in a way which is no different from that of a dog or a very young child. If Annie is to act as a person, if she is to exhibit freedom of the will, then she must reflect on her desire and form a second-order desire: the desire to act on her desire to go to Paris. If she acts without forming that second-order desire, she has, on Frankfurt's view, no stake in the outcome of her action; she is merely the venue in which the interaction of her beliefs and desires takes place, 'a helpless bystander to the forces that move [her]'.[4]

So let us suppose that Annie reflects on her first-order desire to go to Paris, and she thinks to herself that, yes, she would like to act on this desire. She thus forms the second-order desire to act on her desire to go to Paris. She now has a kind of desire which young children and non-human animals cannot have, for they are incapable of reflecting on their first-order desires. This second-order desire, moreover, is unopposed. Annie is not conflicted about the thought of acting on her first-order desire; she has no second thoughts about it whatever. And for precisely this reason, Annie does not stop to reflect on her second-order desire.

But Frankfurt has told us that when a desire is not reflected upon, we have no stake in whether it is effective in producing action. So unless Annie also reflects on this second-order desire, Frankfurt is committed to holding that she still acts wantonly. And, of course, the same will be true should she reflect on her second-order desire, thereby forming a third-order desire to act on it, but fail to reflect, in turn, on that (third-order) desire. An infinite regress results. So long as one's highest-order desire goes unreflected upon, one has no stake, on Frankfurt's view, in whether one acts on it. But however much one reflects, one will inevitably stop somewhere. There will always be some desire which has not itself been reflected upon. And this means that, on Frankfurt's view, wanton behavior is inevitable, and freedom of the will is an impossibility.[5]

The problem here, of course, is exactly parallel to the problems we saw with similar requirements on knowledge and reasoning. There is a

[4] Ibid. 21.

[5] A similar point is made by Gary Watson, 'Free Agency', *Journal of Philosophy*, 72 (1975), 218.

temptation to see reflective assessment as a prerequisite for knowledge, reasoning, and freedom of the will. But on the most straightforward understanding of what this would require, this makes knowledge, reasoning, and freedom of the will impossible to achieve. The temptation is one we will need to resist.

3.2 Higher-order states and alien desires

For reflective people, not all of their desires are on a par. We have all sorts of first-order desires, and some of them are ones we care about a great deal more than others. More than this, some of our first-order desires are ones we wish we did not have, and ones we do not want to be moved by. Frankfurt discusses a case of such an alien desire, a case involving an unwilling addict.

It makes a difference to the unwilling addict, who is a person, which of his conflicting first-order desires wins out. Both desires are his, to be sure; and whether he finally takes the drug or finally succeeds in refraining from taking it, he acts to satisfy what is in a literal sense his own desire. In either case he does something he himself wants to do, and he does it not because of some external influence whose aim happens to coincide with his own but because of his desire to do it. The unwilling addict identifies himself, however, through the formation of a second-order volition, with one rather than with the other of his conflicting first-order desires. He makes one of them more truly his own and, in so doing, he withdraws himself from the other. It is in virtue of this identification and withdrawal, accomplished through the formation of a second-order volition, that the unwilling addict may meaningfully make the analytically puzzling statements that the force moving him to take the drug is a force other than his own, and that it is not of his own free will but rather against his will that this force moves him to take it.[6]

One need not be an addict, of course, to recognize this phenomenon. Anyone who has tried to lose weight, stick to a budget, or simply break themselves of an unwanted habit is familiar with this phenomenon from the inside. We may act on one of our desires—as the unwilling addict does—without that action being a manifestation of free will. When we act on alien desires—desires which are, as Frankfurt rightly insists, nevertheless literally our own—free will does not play a role.

---

[6] Frankfurt, 'Freedom of the Will', 18.

What is definitive of this phenomenon, as Frankfurt sees it, is the having of a second-order state which runs counter to the first-order desire. The unwilling addict wants to have the drug, but also wants not to be moved by that desire, and it is because of this second-order preference that the desire for the drug is seen as alien, and thus any action resulting from the first-order desire fails to manifest free will. First-order desires are thus rightly recognized as ones which do not automatically legitimate action, and Frankfurt's account of what it takes to provide the legitimation involves a second-order state giving its blessing, as it were, to the first-order desire.

This is, I think, quite a natural thought. When we think about the reflective agent, reflecting on his or her many and varied first-order desires, it is tempting to see those first-order desires as separate and apart from the agent, merely accidentally produced within him or her, awaiting legitimation by some act of second-order endorsement. Admittedly, these first-order desires, like the addict's desire for the drug, may be extraordinarily difficult, or even impossible, to get rid of. But how easily one may dispense with a desire tells us nothing about the extent to which it is truly one's own rather than some alien force acting on one. As Frankfurt sees it, the distinction between desires which are alien and those which are truly our own comes down to a distinction between desires which are rejected when we reflect and those which are reflectively endorsed. Actions prompted by first-order desires alone are not free-willed actions. It is actions prompted by those first-order desires which have received a second-order endorsement which count as freely willed.

Once we see that there is a problem of alien desires, however, it should be clear that second-order endorsements cannot possibly confer legitimacy merely in virtue of being higher-order. The problem here is exactly parallel to the problem we confronted about justification and knowledge in Chapter 1. If we are worried about the fact that first-order processes of belief acquisition, allowed to operate without the benefit of reflection, may not all be reliable, then it is no solution to this problem to suggest that we stop to reflect on these first-order processes, adopting beliefs only if they have undergone reflective scrutiny. Reflective scrutiny itself, just like unreflective belief acquisition, need not be reliable. So if one is worried about reliability, as one might legitimately be, one cannot give second-order beliefs a free pass.[7] Second-order beliefs are not immune—either in theory or in practice—to the possibility of being unreliably produced. And the same is true of the kind of second-order endorsements which Frankfurt uses to discriminate between alien desires and those desires which may legitimately be the source of freely willed action: if one is worried about the legitimacy of first-order desires, and the extent to which they are, in some important sense, truly one's own, it simply won't do to adopt the perspective of the reflective agent, take second-order states at face value, and drop all of our worries about legitimacy and ownership merely because we are now dealing with states of a higher order.

Thus, Nomy Arpaly asks us to imagine a reflective agent engaged in the following bit of self-scrutiny.

> I see a piece of cake in the fridge and feel a desire to eat it. But I back up and bring that impulse into view and then I have a certain distance. Now the impulse doesn't dominate me and now I have a problem. Is this desire really a reason to act? I consider the action on its merits and decide that eating the cake is not worth the fat and the calories. I walk away from the fridge . . . [8]

If we have been reading Frankfurt, we might see this as a model of reflective agency and free-willed behavior. The agent has conflicting desires—the desire to eat the cake and the desire to cut down on calories—and, after reflecting, forms a second-order preference to act on the desire to diet. This second-order desire reveals the desire to eat the cake as merely alien, and the action which is informed by the second-order preference to act on the desire to diet as the properly free-willed action.

As Arpaly points out, however, this reflective monologue could be that of a self-possessed agent who freely wills to stick to a diet, or, instead, someone deeply in the grips of anorexia nervosa, rationalizing every act of deprivation as she slowly but systematically starves herself to death.[9] The anorexic does not understand her own motivations, and, indeed, sees herself as a self-possessed agent with a high level of self-understanding

---

[7] Of course, if one is sufficiently optimistic about the reliability of second-order belief acquisition, then one will not see Frankfurt's view as giving second-order beliefs a free pass. We have, however, already seen (in section 1.3 above) a good deal of reason for thinking that such an optimistic view is simply untrue.

[8] *Unprincipled Virtue: An Inquiry into Moral Agency* (Oxford University Press, 2003), 17–18. This passage is modeled, of course, on a passage in Christine Korsgaard, *The Sources of Normativity* (Cambridge University Press, 1996), 93.

[9] *Unprincipled Virtue*, 18.

and self-control. Such an agent is, of course, deeply mistaken about her own psychology, but the truth about herself is not available under conditions of reflection. From the first-person point of view—from the perspective of the reflective agent—there need be no difference at all between the self-controlled dieter who carefully follows a rational plan to lose fifteen pounds and the anorexic who pathologically starves herself to death. But this is just to say, of course, that from the first-person point of view, we are subject to the possibility of profound errors about fundamental features of our own psychology. The fact that action on the basis of a certain desire is endorsed by the reflective agent, that such action is agreeable from the first-person point of view, tells us nothing about which desires are alien and which are truly the agent's own, and it tells us nothing about which actions are freely chosen and which are the product of some sort of compulsion. The first-person point of view, the point of view of the reflective agent, cannot automatically make these distinctions accurately. The mere fact that a psychological state is a higher-order state tells us nothing about its legitimacy or its role in the agent's psychology.

Mental disorders of a great many sorts bring with them a characteristic pattern of self-misunderstanding. Paranoid-schizophrenics, for example, do not, on reflection, recognize that they are victims of paranoia, and when they reflect on their various first-order desires and the actions open to them, the (second-order) preferences they form about which of their first-order desires will be effective in producing action are themselves influenced by their paranoia.[10] When they are unreflective, their behavior can be the product of various compulsions they are subject to, but a reflective turn does not, of course, allow them to bypass these compulsions. Their second-order desires to act on certain first-order desires seem as rational to them as yours and mine seem to us. But this is not to say, of course, that paranoid-schizophrenics have a great deal of self-understanding, or that they act rationally, or that their second-order preferences serve to distinguish alien desires from desires which are truly their own, or that they act in a manner which exhibits freedom of the will when their second-order volitions properly line up with the first-order beliefs which actually move them. None of these things, of course, are true. Like the anorexic, the paranoid schizophrenic has an interior monologue which

[10] See *Diagnostic and Statistical Manual of Mental Disorders* (*DSM-IV*), 4th edn. (American Psychiatric Association, 1994), 274–88.

appears quite rational, and which mirrors the interior monologue of the self-possessed reflective agent. But the appearance of being self-possessed is part of the problem that such individuals face. One cannot appeal to features of the first-person perspective, or the reflective agent, in order to distinguish those who are self-possessed, or who are acting freely, or who are exhibiting freedom of the will, from those who are not.

Nor is it necessary to choose examples here which involve mental disorders. We all, at times, fail to fully understand our own motives. We are all, at times, moved in ways we do not fully understand. And we all, at times, engage in sincere acts of rationalization. We may be moved to act by first-order desires in ways which are irrational and not fully free, and yet, at the same time, when we reflect on these desires, like the anorexic or the paranoid schizophrenic, we may form a second-order preference to be moved by them. The very irrationality which prompted the first-order desire may serve as a motive for rationalization when we turn reflective. The psychology of self-deceived reflective agents should not be conflated with the psychology of those who are utterly self-possessed.

Once we see that the concerns about the origins of first-order desires may equally apply to second-order states, it becomes clear not only that second-order endorsements are not sufficient for free-willed action (since the second-order endorsement itself may have a heritage which undermines any legitimating role it might otherwise play). It also becomes clear that a failure of fit between second- and first-order states need not, automatically, be taken to reflect badly on the states of lower order. There are, of course, unwilling addicts, just as Frankfurt describes, who are compelled to act by first-order desires which they do not want to be moved by; such agents, as Frankfurt rightly urges, do not act in a way that exhibits free will. But we should not think that whenever an agent acts on a first-order desire in the face of a second-order desire not to be moved by it, that this too must be a case of action which is not freely willed.

Arpaly, again, is instructive here. Consider her reconstruction of the incident in Mark Twain's *The Adventures of Huckleberry Finn* in which Finn fails to turn in Jim, an escaped slave.[11] Although Finn can't bring himself to turn Jim in, he believes that what he is doing is wrong, and he berates himself for behaving immorally. Although Twain (unsurprisingly) does

---

[11] For a different, and, to my mind, far less plausible, reconstruction of this story, see Jonathan Bennett, 'The Conscience of Huck Finn', *Philosophy*, 49 (1974), 123–34.

not describe it in these terms, we might even imagine that Finn forms the second-order desire not to be moved by his first-order desire that Jim remain free. As Arpaly describes the case:

Talking to Jim about his hopes and fears and interacting with him extensively, Huckleberry constantly perceives data (never deliberated upon) that amount to the message that Jim is a person, just like him. Twain makes it very easy for Huckleberry to perceive the similarity between himself and Jim: the two are equally ignorant, share the same language and superstitions, and all in all it does not take the genius of John Stuart Mill to see that there is no particular reason to think of one of them as inferior to the other. While Huckleberry never reflects on these facts, they do prompt him to act toward Jim, more and more, in the same way he would have acted toward any other friend. That Huckleberry begins to perceive Jim as a fellow human being becomes clear when Huckleberry finds himself, to his surprise, *apologizing* to Jim—an action unthinkable in a society that treats black men as something less than human.[12]

As Arpaly argues, Finn is moved by a moral motivation, and his first-order desire that Jim remain free is not merely due to some sort of personal sympathy in the face of (however misguided) moral reasons to the contrary. Finn's first-order preferences are anything but alien; they are not mere compulsions which move him against his will. It is, instead, his second-order beliefs and preferences which are alien and defective. As Arpaly points out, Finn 'is not a very clear abstract thinker'.[13] His second-order belief, about the moral acceptability of his motives, for example, and his second-order preference, to be moved by certain desires, are themselves rather shallow, not deeply rooted in his character in the way that his appreciation of Jim's personhood is. For that very reason, these second-order states are badly suited for playing the role of discriminating between alien and legitimating first-order desires; they cannot be the determinants of which actions are freely willed.

Finn's failure to be moved reliably by abstract reasons when he engages in reflection, despite his ability, at the first-order level, to respond reliably to reasons, is neither mysterious nor uncommon. The ability to articulate one's reasons in any detail, even to oneself on reflection, is a highly specialized skill, one which requires a good deal of education and training. Thinking about reasons qua reasons is especially abstract, and it is something which does not come naturally even to many who have a good deal

---

[12] Arpaly, *Unprincipled Virtue*, 77.   [13] Ibid.

of education. After all, a good deal of education does not focus on the nature of reasons qua reasons. But this is not to say that, without such an abstract focus, one's first-order beliefs and preferences cannot be moved by reason. We are, after all, very frequently responsive to factors of which we are only dimly aware, and which we can only articulate in the vaguest terms. As we saw in Chapter 2, reliably responding to reasons does not require a second-order understanding of those reasons, or even the ability to form the concept of a reason. We may thus succeed in responding to reasons at the first-order level while failing to identify, or even respond to them, in our second-order reflections. We should not think that it is only at the second-order level that we engage with reasons, or even that, on those occasions when we are prompted to engage in second-order reflections, their second-order character gives them some automatic connection with reasons.

The same is true of the connection between second-order reflections and freely willed actions. It cannot be, as the infinite regress shows, that higher-order reflection is a necessary condition of free-willed action, at least if free-willed action is to be a genuine possibility. Nor can it be, given the nature of our psychology, that reflection somehow serves automatically to discriminate alien desires from those which are truly our own. The problems which beset first-order thinking and action are ones which may arise at the second-order level as well. By the same token, the kind of engagement we seek, in both our beliefs and our actions, require no special second-order endorsement.

3.3 Epistemic agency

Issues about the role of reflection in agency come to the fore in discussions of epistemic agency. The idea that there is such a thing as epistemic agency deserves, I believe, a good deal of examination.

Most of the time, we form beliefs unreflectively. If our eyes are open and there is a table directly in front of us in good light and perfectly normal circumstances, we will come to believe that a table is there. We don't stop to reflect about whether things are really as they seem, nor do we stop to consider whether the belief we thereby form is genuinely justified. These questions could, of course, occur to us, but in the ordinary course of events, they simply do not occur. Our eyes are open; we see the table; we come to believe that the table is there. In cases like this, beliefs seem to be arrived at passively. They are no more chosen than are the visual sensations which the table causes.

But not all belief is like this. We do, at times, stop to reflect. 'Is this what I ought to believe?' we ask ourselves. We deliberate. We consciously entertain alternative views, and we think about which, if any, belief about the situation before us we are justified in holding. In situations like this, we seem to play a more active role. We don't just find ourselves believing things. Rather, we decide what to believe; we make up our minds; we choose to believe one thing rather than another. It is in situations such as this that we may be tempted to talk of *epistemic agency*.

Thus, for example, in *Freedom of the Individual*, Stuart Hampshire remarks:

'What do I believe?' turns into the question 'What ought to be believed?,' for the man who asks the question; but not necessarily for his audience, if he has one. The audience may be interested in the fact that I believe so-and-so: but for me this is not a fact that I learn, except in very abnormal cases . . . it is normally a decision, a making up of one's mind, rather than a discovery, a discovery about one's mind.[14]

This idea that, at least when we reflect, our beliefs are typically formed by way of a decision, and our knowledge of our beliefs in these situations is to be explained by the fact that we decided what to believe rather than by any discovery we might make about our minds, is absolutely central to Richard Moran's account of self-knowledge in *Authority and Estrangement*.[15] In commenting on the passage quoted above, Moran remarks:

Hampshire is not endorsing a voluntarism about belief here, as if one's beliefs were normally picked out and adopted at will. The agency a person exercises with respect to his beliefs and other attitudes is obviously not like that of overt basic actions like reaching for a glass.[16]

But this, of course, raises a puzzle. If Hampshire, and Moran following him, wish to insist that we are agents with respect to our beliefs, that there is, in short, genuine epistemic agency, then how are we to make sense of this idea if it is not by way of some sort of voluntarism about belief?

[14] *Freedom of the Individual* (Chatto & Windus, 1965), 75–6.
[15] *Authority and Estrangement* (Princeton University Press, 2001).
[16] Ibid. 114.

Hampshire and Moran are not alone here. Voluntarism about belief is not a very widely held position,[17] but the appeal to epistemic agency is, indeed, quite widespread. Thus, Christine Korsgaard claims:

the human mind *is* self-conscious in the sense that it is essentially reflective . . . A lower animal's attention is fixed on the world. Its perceptions are its beliefs and its desires are its will . . . But we human animals turn our attention on to our perceptions and desires themselves, on to our own mental activities, and we are conscious *of* them.

And this sets us a problem no other animal has. It is the problem of the normative. For our capacity to turn our attention on to our own mental activities is also a capacity to distance ourselves from them, and to call them into question. I perceive, and I find myself with a powerful impulse to believe. But I back up and bring that impulse into view and then I have a certain distance. Now the impulse doesn't dominate me and now I have a problem. Shall I believe? Is this perception really a *reason* to believe? . . . The reflective mind cannot settle for perception and desire, not just as such. It needs a *reason*. Otherwise, at least as long as it reflects, it cannot commit itself or go forward.[18]

On this picture, we may certainly form beliefs unreflectively, as lower animals do, and then our belief formation is entirely passive. But when we reflect on our situation, we cannot come to form beliefs without making a commitment; some genuine activity on our part is required. It is thus when we reflect that we exercise our epistemic agency. Korsgaard goes on:

The problem can also be described in terms of freedom. It is because of the reflective character of the mind that we must act, as Kant put it, under the idea of freedom.[19]

Unreflective belief does not involve free choice; it is not active; it is not something we do. But when we reflect, we make a choice as to what to believe. We are not passive. We are epistemic agents.

We see the same themes come to the fore in Ernest Sosa's work. In *A Virtue Epistemology*,[20] there is an analogy which runs throughout. Sosa begins the book with the example of an archer shooting at a target. Sosa

---

[17] But see Carl Ginet, 'Deciding to Believe', in Matthias Steup (ed.), *Knowledge, Truth, and Duty* (Oxford University Press, 2001), 63–76; Sharon Ryan, 'Doxastic Compatibilism and the Ethics of Belief', *Philosophical Studies*, 114 (2003), 47–79; Matthias Steup, 'Doxastic Freedom', *Synthese*, 161 (2008), 375–92.

[18] Korsgaard, *The Sources of Normativity* (Cambridge University Press, 1996), 92–3.

[19] Ibid. 94.

[20] Sosa, *A Virtue Epistemology* (Oxford University Press, 2007).

remarks that the archer's performance, like all performances, may be assessed along three different dimensions. We may ask whether it was accurate (i.e. whether it succeeded in its aim); whether it was adroit (i.e. whether it manifested a skill); and whether it was apt (i.e. assuming it was both accurate and adroit, whether it was accurate as a result of being adroit). Sosa refers to this as the 'AAA structure'. He then goes on to say, 'Beliefs fall under the AAA structure, as do performances generally.'[21] But there is certainly something puzzling about this. Beliefs don't seem to be performances. They are not actions. They do not seem to be something that we do.

Sosa gives a very brief response to this worry. He comments,

Some acts are performances, of course, but so are some sustained states. Think of those live motionless statues that one sees at tourist sites. Such performances can linger, and need not be constantly sustained through renewed conscious intentions. The performer's mind could wander, with little effect on the continuation or quality of the performance.[22]

But this does not really respond to the concern. The worry is not about whether there is a *conscious* intention at work here. The worry is about whether there is any intention at all. The performer who remains motionless is clearly doing so as a result of an intention. No one can remain as motionless as these performers do without intending to do so. But believers, at least typically, do not form beliefs as a result of an intention. At least typically, when I look at a table in front of me and come to form the belief that there is a table, I am not moved by any intention, conscious or otherwise, any more than my dog is moved by an intention to form a belief when he comes to believe that there is food in his dish. So the suggestion that we may see belief formation, like the shooting of an arrow, as a kind of performance seems to be just a mistake.

We may, perhaps, however, better see what it is that Sosa has in mind by returning to the issue raised in section 1.4 about the value of reflection. What is it about reflection, and beliefs formed under the guidance of reflection, that makes it so important, according to Sosa? One part of Sosa's answer to this question involves epistemic agency:

reflection aids agency, control of conduct by the whole person, not just by peripheral modules. When reasons are in conflict, as they so often are, not only in deliberation but in theorizing, and not only in the higher reaches of theoretical science but in the most ordinary reasoning about matters of fact, we need a way holistically to strike a balance, which would seem to import an assessment of the respective weights of pros and cons, all of which evidently is played out through perspective on one's attitudes and the bearing of those various reasons.[23]

So, once again, we see a connection being made between reflective belief formation and agency. My unreflective belief which simply registers the presence of the table, like my dog's unreflective belief which registers the presence of his food, is merely passive. But when I stop to reflect—something my dog cannot do—I become an agent with respect to my beliefs. Like Hampshire, Moran, and Korsgaard, Sosa believes that human beings are epistemic agents, and our agency comes into play when we form beliefs reflectively.[24]

A commitment to the existence of genuine epistemic agency is thus quite central to the work of a number of philosophers, philosophers who differ dramatically in other respects. The notion of epistemic agency, however, deserves more scrutiny than it has thus far received.[25]

3.4 Mechanism and epistemic agency

What, after all, is the view of cognition which is implicit in these sugges-tions? Consider, first, the case of unreflective belief acquisition. The mechanisms at work in a person which produce beliefs of any sort, including unreflective belief, are extraordinarily complex. They are not, for the most part, available to introspection. When I form perceptual beliefs, for example, my perceptual apparatus engages in a process of edge-detection which is made possible by way of mechanisms which are responsive to sudden changes in illumination across my visual field.[26] These mechanisms operate sub-personally. They are, as Sosa puts it,

---

[23] 'Replies', in John Greco (ed.), *Ernest Sosa and his Critics* (Blackwell, 2004), 292.

[24] It is for this reason, no doubt, that Sosa thinks that belief formation may, at least at times, when it is apt, be something a person deserves credit for. (See *A Virtue Epistemology*, ch. 5.) The notion of credit at work here is not merely the notion of causal responsibility, as when the proper spelling of a certain word in some text is 'credited' to the automatic operation of a spell checking program. Talk of credit in this context is far more substantive, as befits a virtue-theoretic approach.

[25] An exception here lies in two important papers by John Heil: 'Doxastic Agency', *Philosophical Studies*, 43 (1983), 355–64, and 'Doxastic Incontinence', *Mind*, 93 (1984), 56–70.

[26] See e.g. David Marr, *Vision* (W. H. Freeman, 1982).

'peripheral modules'. Edge-detection is not something which I engage in, at least in standard cases of perception; rather, it is something done by sub-personal mechanisms within me. Here, at least, I do not act. Mechanisms within me are at work which simply produce perceptual beliefs.

How then are things supposed to be different when I engage in reflection? It will be best to have a simple example before us. Suppose that I am serving on a jury in which someone is charged with murder. Imagine as well that I don't simply react to the evidence presented. Instead, I stop to reflect. I self-consciously consider whether the evidence presented supports a guilty verdict. Here, when I stop to reflect, is where epistemic agency is supposed to be found. But where, precisely, does my agency come into play?

There certainly are things that I do in the course of reflecting on the evidence presented at trial. I may focus my attention on various pieces of evidence and question their relevance as well as their probity. The focusing of my attention is arguably something that I do, as is the activity of questioning both the relevance and the probity of the evidence. So there is genuine agency at work here, at least if we accept these commonsense accounts of what is going on.[27] But activities of this sort, while they are certainly present when a person reflects on his or her beliefs, are no different in kind from various activities we all engage in when forming unreflective beliefs. Thus, for example, just as I focus my attention on various bits of evidence when I carry out my jury duties, I turn my head in the direction I wish to look when I form various perceptual beliefs. Turning my head is certainly a voluntary activity; it is a manifestation of my agency. But the fact that I turn my head voluntarily does not show that my perceptual belief itself is a manifestation of epistemic agency—as all of

---

[27] I don't believe that we should accept these commonsense accounts of our mental lives. Indeed, the history of the cognitive sciences over the last fifty years seems to me to show very clearly that the phenomenology of mental processes is not even roughly reliable in producing an understanding of the mechanisms which actually operate. It is not just that the phenomenology leaves out important features of those mechanisms. Rather, even when it comes to those features of the mechanisms which the phenomenology represents, it very often misrepresents their role. For a recent defense of this view, see Timothy Wilson, *Strangers to Ourselves: Discovering the Adaptive Unconscious* (Harvard University Press, 2002). I take the commonsensical view at face value in the text here, however, not because I believe it to be correct, but rather because I believe that it presents the best possible case in favor of epistemic agency. Certainly none of the authors under discussion here defend their views on the basis of empirical work in psychology.

agency. When we look at belief acquisition from the first-person perspective, however, there is, at least, the appearance of agency. What should we make of the difference which these two perspectives offer us?

Richard Moran suggests that the first-person perspective cannot simply be explained away as some sort of illusion: 'a non-empirical or transcendental relation to the self is ineliminable'.[28] There is a special authority which we have over our beliefs that is revealed to us, on Moran's view, from the first-person perspective, and it is here that our epistemic agency may be found. As Moran sees it:

> This is a form of authority tied to the presuppositions of rational agency and is different in kind from the more purely epistemic authority that may attach to the special immediacy of the person's access to his mental life.[29]

We may begin to understand what it is that Moran has in mind here by looking at his discussion of an example from Sartre. Consider the case of a habitual and chronic gambler who vows to give up his gambling. The gambler may examine his own past behavior from the third-person point of view and, given his many unsuccessful attempts to reform, question whether he is really able to follow through on his present resolve. But the gambler must also simply decide what it is that he is going to do. As Moran sees it:

> There is one kind of evasion in the empty denial of one's facticity (e.g., one's history of weakness and fallibility), as if to say 'Don't worry about my actual history of letting you down, for I hereby renounce and transcend all that.' But there is also evasion in submerging oneself in facticity, as if to say, 'Of course, whether I will in fact disappoint you again is a fully empirical question. You know as much as I do as to what the probabilities are, and so you can plan accordingly.'[30]

There is no question that we would feel little confidence in someone who, after telling of his resolve to stop gambling, reminded us that he has resolved to do this many times before, with little success. Someone who says this is not only reminding us of relevant information. Such a person seems to be preparing us for his own failure so as to ensure that, should we depend on him to stop gambling and find that we have been disappointed, we will have no one to blame but ourselves. When he returns to the

---

[28] Moran, *Authority and Estrangement*, 90.   [29] Ibid. 92.   [30] Ibid. 81.

gaming tables, he is now in a position to say, 'I told you so', despite his avowed commitment to quit.

So Moran is surely right that there are two different kinds of evasion to be found here. But what are we to make of this? We might well think that the gambler who both insists that he is going to quit, and, at the same time, reminds us of his history of backsliding on such decisions, is doing more than just undermining our confidence that he will follow through with his decision. Some people in situations like this do in fact follow through on their resolve; many others do not. But surely someone who keeps focusing on his history of failure, rather than focusing on his resolve to quit, makes it more likely that he will fail. We may reasonably think that the gambler who insists, 'This time I'm really going to quit', is overly optimistic. But such a person has a degree of resolve which is probably necessary (even if not sufficient) for dealing with the inevitable temptations to follow, and the person who is focused on his past failures is missing this.

Consider the approach of Alcoholics Anonymous (AA) in dealing with similar concerns.[31] Those who wish to give up their problem drinking are encouraged to believe that their resolution to quit may carry them through the various temptations that they will face, and they are encouraged to believe that, in facing such temptations, it is not their resolution alone which will allow for their success; there is no attempt here to deny their 'facticity', for example, by suggesting that their prior history of backsliding is irrelevant. Rather, AA encourages their members to believe that, in moments of temptation, they may surrender to a 'higher power' who will help them through. It is this that will make the difference over past failed attempts.

Now I don't mean to be suggesting that the success which Alcoholics Anonymous has shown in dealing with the difficulties of giving up alcohol is best explained by the existence of such a higher power. This would not, I acknowledge, be one of the more persuasive arguments for the existence of a deity. But while AA should not be deferred to on matters of theology, it does seem to me that they display a fine understanding of human psychology. The twin temptations for evasion which Moran nicely identifies are both sidestepped in their approach. They do not deny that a knowledge of one's history of backsliding is important for the alcoholic,

---

[31] See http://www.alcoholics-anonymous.org/en_information_aa.cfm

but they work on focusing the would-be quitter's attention elsewhere, and on developing that person's resolve to quit, while simultaneously instilling beliefs which prepare that person for the challenges and temptations which he or she will inevitably face.

Just as we should not take AA's invocation of a 'higher power' at face value, Moran's suggestion that there is some sort of 'transcendental or non-empirical relation to the self' at work here need not be taken at face value. The gambler in Sartre's example who can do no more than focus on his past history of failure, even while intermittently avowing that he is going to quit, need not be seen as lacking some non-empirical relationship to his self, a relationship which can only be revealed to the first-person perspective. A third-person perspective is all that is needed to appreciate the difference between such a person and the sincere and successful member of Alcoholics Anonymous, as well as those highly motivated individuals who give up bad habits and addictions by other means. Focusing on a history of failure doesn't alienate one from a transcendental self. It merely undermines some of the more effective empirical mechanisms for changing behavior.

The cases of the gambler and the alcoholic involve actions, rather than beliefs. But, as Moran points out, the same issues arise in the case of belief.

With respect to beliefs, the parallel asymmetry would be the instability in the idea of trust or mistrust being applied to one's own belief, in the sense of treating the empirical fact of one's *having* the belief as evidence for its truth. If a generally reliable person believes that it's raining out, that fact *can* certainly be treated as evidence for rain. But in my own case, as with the resolution not to gamble, I must recognize that the belief is mine to retain or to abandon. . . . That is, my belief only exists as an empirical psychological fact insofar as I *am* persuaded by the evidence for rain, evidence which (prior to my belief) does not include the fact of my being persuaded. If I am unpersuaded enough to need additional evidence, then by virtue of that psychological fact itself I lose the empirical basis for any inference from a person's belief to the truth about the rain. For someone's *un*confident belief about the rain provides much less reason for anyone to take it to be good evidence for rain itself.[32]

Moran is certainly right that this kind of case is interesting, but it is not at all clear what it shows. Let us take an example which is slightly more fleshed out. Suppose that Jane is a physician and, after extensive examination of a patient together with a careful scrutiny of a wide range of test results, she comes to believe, somewhat tentatively, that the patient has a certain

---

[32] Moran, *Authority and Estrangement*, 83.

disease. If Jane is a reliable diagnostician, then we should take this fact about her diagnosis, i.e. this fact about what she believes, to be good evidence that the patient has that very disease. As Moran rightly points out, however, there would certainly be something odd about Jane herself using this fact about her belief as evidence for its truth.

But why, precisely, is that so? Suppose that Jane discusses this case with her colleague Mary, someone who knows that Jane has an excellent track record as a diagnostician. Jane has had these talks with Mary before, and Mary has come to two conclusions about these conversations. First, Jane is often a bit tentative in the diagnoses she makes; she does not have the same degree of confidence in her diagnoses that many of their other colleagues do. But, second, Jane is much more frequently right than her other colleagues are; she has a superb record as a diagnostician, even when her diagnoses are tentative. Indeed, although she typically expresses (quite sincerely) a good deal of caution about her diagnoses, she very rarely has reason, subsequently, to modify them.

Now in a situation like this, I believe that Mary should come to the belief that Jane's diagnosis is correct. The track record evidence, including a track record in conditions in which Jane's diagnosis is tentative, provides strong evidence for the correctness of the diagnosis. And Moran would certainly agree. But now imagine Mary giving Jane the following pep talk:

> Jane, you're a wonderful diagnostician. Your track record of making accurate diagnoses is remarkable. You've done all the relevant tests and scrutinized them carefully. And when you've done this in the past, you've always been very tentative in your conclusions, but they're almost always right. There's nothing different about this case. You should be a great deal more confident than you are. If you think this patient has that disease, then there's excellent reason to believe that he does.

It seems to me that Jane should be convinced by this bit of reasoning, and, if she is, then what she would be doing is using the fact that she believes as evidence for its own truth, in just the way that Mary, and everyone else, uses the fact that Jane has reached a certain conclusion as reason to believe that very conclusion. This bit of reasoning is perfectly good when others use it. It is no less good reason if Jane is convinced by it as well. Indeed, this third-person approach to her own reasoning may be used, as Mary encourages her to do, as a way of apportioning her beliefs to the evidence. Before Jane considers her own track record of successful diagnosis and her own tendency to be more tentative than she should, she is, in this case, as in others before, underestimating the strength of her evidence. By focusing on the fact that she has some small degree of confidence in her diagnosis, and her track record in such situations, she may raise her own degree of confidence in just the way she ought. This may involve a third-person perspective on her own beliefs, but it is none the worse for that. If this involves being alienated from oneself as a believer, then there's nothing wrong with such alienation. And if taking the first-person perspective on one's beliefs prevents one from viewing them in the way Jane does after the pep talk from Mary, then the first-person perspective can thereby get in the way of good cognitive self-management. Indeed, perhaps it would do us all a bit of good if we were alienated from our own beliefs in just this way a good deal more often.[33]

Once again we are led to ask: just where is the agency involved in belief acquisition supposed to be found? What reason is there for believing that there is such a thing as epistemic agency? At one point, Moran suggests that we may see the workings of epistemic agency whenever we criticize someone's reasons for belief.

Without the understanding that the person you're speaking to is in a position to exercise some effective agency here, there would be no point in criticizing his reasoning on some point since otherwise what would *he*, the person you're talking to, have to do with either the process or the outcome? He might be in a superior position to view the results of your intervention ('from the inside,' as it were), but both of you would have to simply await the outcome. Instead, it seems clear that the very possibility of ordinary argument (and other discourse) presumes that the reasons he accepts and the conclusion he draws are 'up to him' in the relevant sense.[34]

But it is not at all clear why the discussion of reasons, and the offering of arguments, presumes any sort of agency at all. When we offer people reasons for believing some proposition, or reasons for changing one of their beliefs, we certainly do take for granted that they are capable of being moved by reasons. We don't offer reasons to a tree stump. But it is one thing to say that people are capable of being moved by reason or that they are responsive to reason; it is quite another to insist that they are genuine

---

[33] Needless to say, the need for adjustment due to overconfidence is almost certainly a larger problem in practice. For discussion of this issue within a Bayesian framework, see Sherrilyn Roush, 'Second Guessing: A Self-Help Manual', *Episteme*, forthcoming.

[34] Moran, *Authority and Estrangement*, 119–20.

epistemic agents. Moran suggests that if we view belief acquisition in a way which divorces it from agency, then when we offer someone reasons for belief, 'we would have to simply await the outcome'. But we don't, at least in many cases, need to wait at all simply because the wheels of the reasoning mechanism turn rather quickly. If you and I disagree about the sum of two numbers, and then, when you look over my calculations, you point out a simple error I've made, you needn't wait for me to acknowledge my mistake. But this is not because I acted as an agent upon my beliefs; it is because my reasoning mechanism is sensitive to the point you raised, and, given the obviousness of the error, my belief is quickly adjusted. I don't have to do anything once you point the error out to me. My reasoning mechanism does the work for me.

Of course, not all disagreements are so easily resolved. You may disagree with me on some complex issue, and, although you do in fact point out an error which I've made, the precise upshot of the error is not immediately obvious to me. Sometimes the reasoning mechanism operates more slowly. And in these cases, contrary to what Moran suggests, we do both need to wait to see what I end up believing.

Moran suggests that there is something wrong with any picture of belief acquisition which robs it of agency because, in offering someone reasons to change his belief, we must, somehow, assume that belief is up to him. If we don't assume this, Moran argues, 'what would *he*, the person you're talking to, have to do with either the process or the outcome?' But I take it that we offer reasons to individuals precisely because we believe that the individuals themselves don't have anything to do with the outcome. When all is working as it should, our belief acquisition mechanisms are simply responsive to reason. We don't have to engage these mechanisms, or decide what to do with their output. Their output just is a belief, and thus no action on our part is required.

What we believe, when all is going well, has nothing to do with what we want, and this is precisely why the reasoning mechanisms may operate so well. Our wants have nothing to do with the reasons we have for belief, at least in the typical case; belief formation which involved agency, and thus allowed our desires to play a role in the beliefs we form, would thus pervert the process. Thus, when we offer others reasons for belief, we assume just the opposite of what Moran suggests: we assume that, to a first approximation, the desires of the people we are talking to will have nothing to do with what they come to believe. They will only be moved by reasons, and thus, their agency will play no role in the beliefs they acquire.

Of course, individuals are not perfectly responsive to reason, and we know this. When we offer reasons for belief, however confident we may be that we are in the right, we do not just assume that our interlocutors will come to share our views. In simple cases, such as the arithmetic mistake, we can safely assume, at least for most interlocutors, that they will simply respond, and respond appropriately, to the reasons offered. But the more complex the reasoning offered, the more room there is for an otherwise rational individual to fail to respond to reasons. Reasoning mechanisms, like all manner of mechanisms, are subject to interfering factors, and even when they operate without interference, they need not always operate properly. Even in otherwise rational individuals, there may be both performance failures and failures of competence. But whether the reasoning mechanisms are operating well or badly, we need not, and do not, assume that the individual to whom reasons are offered will exert any agency with respect to his or her beliefs.

These considerations, it seems, do not provide us with convincing reasons to believe that there really is such a thing as epistemic agency. But we will need to revisit these issues in a somewhat different guise.

3.6 Epistemic agency and deliberation

There is another idea about where and how our epistemic agency best reveals itself: it arises, again, in the course of deliberation about what to believe. When we stop to think about what to believe, we must, some argue, regard ourselves as agents. Thus, Korsgaard remarks that: 'It is because of the reflective character of the mind that we must act, as Kant put it, under the idea of freedom.'[35] And Moran has a similar view:

The basic point can be expressed in a loosely Kantian style, although the idea is hardly unique to Kant. The stance from which a person speaks with any special authority about his belief or his action is not a stance of causal explanation but the stance of rational agency.... It is an expression of the authority of reason here that he can and must answer the question of his belief or action by reflection on the reasons in favor of this belief or action. To do otherwise would be for him to take the course of his belief or his intentional action to be up to something other than his sense of the best reasons, and if he thinks *that*, then there's no point in his deliberating about what

[35] Korsgaard, *Sources of Normativity*, 94.

to do. Indeed, there is no point in calling it 'deliberation' any more, if he takes it to be an open question whether this activity will determine what he actually does or believes. To engage in deliberation in the first place is to hand over the question of one's belief or intentional action to the authority of reason.[36]

So on this view, deliberation itself, if it is to be properly so-called, requires that we regard ourselves as free agents in the course of our deliberation. Now even if this were so, there would be a further question we would need to ask. Perhaps we need to regard ourselves as agents in order to engage in deliberation, but the question we were concerned with was not whether we need to think of ourselves as agents when we deliberate, but whether we genuinely are epistemic agents. So even if there is some necessity in regarding oneself as an epistemic agent, we might still reasonably ask whether that view we have of ourselves, when we deliberate about what to believe, is an accurate one. But we need not pursue this issue here, for, as I will argue, it is not even true that we need to regard ourselves in the way that Kant, Korsgaard, and Moran suggest that we do.[37]

There are two suggestions which Moran makes in the passage quoted above, and, although he regards them as linked, I believe it is important to keep them separate. First, he suggests that deliberation involves agency, or, as he puts it in this passage, 'rational agency'. And second, he suggests that in the course of deliberation, we must regard our beliefs as being handed over to 'the authority of reason'. Now while Moran regards these claims as complementary, it seems to be that they are, in fact, in tension with one another. In my view, we should accept (a qualified version of) the second claim, but we should reject the first.

We may certainly regard our beliefs, under deliberation, as ones which are given over to the authority of reason. We reflect, after all, in the belief that this will allow us to better determine the truth, and we believe that our faculty of reason, if this is the way to put it, will be instrumental in producing true beliefs, or at least in increasing the likelihood that we arrive at true

---

[36] Moran, *Authority and Estrangement*, 127.

[37] This argument for epistemic agency is, of course, quite similar to the widely made argument for the claim that, insofar as we deliberate about what to do, we must regard ourselves as free agents and, on some views, that the very fact of deliberation therefore shows that we are free agents. For a useful discussion of this argument, see Derk Pereboom, *Living without Free Will* (Cambridge University Press, 2001), 135–9.

beliefs.[38] But this is perfectly compatible with the view that there is no such thing as epistemic agency. Indeed, it is compatible with the view that when we deliberate, we do not even believe that we are epistemic agents.

Why should we think, then, that we need even to regard ourselves as epistemic agents when we deliberate about what to believe? Consider, for a moment, an analogy. Think of the behavior of airport security personnel screening prospective passengers before they are allowed to proceed to the departure gates. Passengers are sometimes 'wanded', that is, the screener will use a hand-held metal detector, or wand, to determine whether the passenger might be carrying a gun or a knife. The wand is systematically passed over the passenger's body, and if some sufficiently large or dense metal object is detected, the wand emits a loud tone. These wands are quite reliable, and the security personnel come to trust them a great deal.

Now when passengers are screened in this manner, the screeners are engaged in a voluntary, intentional activity. They freely decide where the wand is to be held, and they go out of their way to try to focus on areas where guns or knives might be hidden. The wand will sometimes emit a tentative-sounding tone, either when it is in the vicinity of a small metal object (such as a belt-buckle) or when it is a bit further away from a larger or denser metal object (such as a knife or gun), and when the wand emits this tentative sound, the screener will slow down and focus the wand on the area which provoked the response.

In screening passengers in this way, there is an intentional activity—the manipulation of the wand—and there is as well, as a crucial part of the screening, the thoroughly mechanical action of the wand itself. While the screener has control over where the wand is held, the behavior of the wand is not subject to the screener's will. The wand will beep when it is close to something metal, whatever the screener may have in mind. Indeed, the wand can only work effectively—especially given the inattentive way in which some screeners approach their job—if it does behave in a way which is insulated from the screener's intentions.

Deliberation about what to believe, it seems, works in a similar way. There are, beyond doubt, certain activities which we engage in in the course of deliberation. We focus our attention on certain questions or

---

[38] This is, as we have seen in section 1.3, an overly optimistic view of what actually happens during deliberation, but I don't deny that it is a view which is widely held.

pieces of evidence; we may decide to look for additional evidence before we proceed further. The possibility of proceeding in these ways may well require not only our agency, but a recognition of our own agency. But we are agents here in the same way that the screeners are agents in deciding where the wand is to be held. And just as the wand has a life of its own, as it were, operating in ways which are insensitive to our intentions, the operation of our inferential mechanisms is similarly insensitive to our agency. We direct our attention in various ways, and our inferential mechanisms then go to work. We are able to have confidence in our deliberation, just as the screeners have confidence in their searches, to the extent that we regard our reasoning mechanisms, like the wands, as reliable. And, as I've emphasized, that reliability can only be had if it is purchased at the price of being insulated from our agency.

Beliefs under deliberation thus seem to be no more a product of epistemic agency than are beliefs formed unreflectively. Our agency plays a part in belief acquisition, but not in a way which legitimizes talk of epistemic agency.

3.7 Epistemic agency and epistemic responsibility

All of the authors under discussion here connect the idea of epistemic agency with reflection, and we have therefore been considering whether there is reason to believe that reflective belief acquisition is different in kind from unreflective belief acquisition, with the former exhibiting agency while the latter does not. There seems, however, to be no such difference. While unreflective belief acquisition does seem to be, in relevant respects, entirely passive, reflective belief acquisition seems to be no different.

But this may be the wrong way to view how the appeal to reflection ought to be understood. Thus, for example, when Sosa introduces the distinction between animal knowledge and reflective knowledge, it might seem that while non-human animals are capable of nothing but animal knowledge,[39] human beings sometimes have mere animal knowledge (for we very often form beliefs unreflectively) and sometimes have reflective knowledge. But this is not what Sosa says. Right after drawing the

---

[39] At least if we assume, plausibly, that they are incapable of reflection.

distinction, he remarks: 'Note that no human blessed with reason has merely animal knowledge of the sort attainable by beasts.'[40] So human knowledge is viewed as different in kind from animal knowledge even on those occasions when we form beliefs unreflectively. The important dividing line thus seems to be the one between the beliefs of humans (who are capable of reflection) and the beliefs of non-human animals (who are not), rather than the one between reflective belief acquisition and unreflective belief acquisition.

How might we flesh this out so as to underwrite an account of epistemic agency? The account I offer here is not one which I would attribute to any individual. While it is inspired by a number of comments in Sosa's text, as well as by the remarks of a number of the Sellarsian philosophers discussed in Chapter 2, it is certainly not something to which anyone explicitly commits himself. At the same time, I think that this view is well worth taking seriously, whether it may be attributed to Sosa, or the Sellarsians, or not. It is, I believe, an account which many will find attractive, and it may well underlie the way at least many of us are tempted to think about some of the differences between human and non-human cognition. Indeed, I believe that the suggestion I offer here may have a good deal more initial plausibility than the variations on Kantian themes we have so far considered, even if, in the end, I will argue that it should be rejected.

Sosa presents his view as a virtue epistemology, and we may usefully begin by asking what it is about human belief acquisition which lends itself to some sort of virtue account in a way that non-human animal belief acquisition does not. Some might suggest, as we have seen that Michael Williams does,[41] that one important difference here is that, even if animals are properly regarded as having beliefs, the manner in which they form beliefs simply does not change over time. Their processes of belief acquisition are hard-wired, and, even if these processes are, for many purposes, quite reliable, and thus capable of producing (at least a kind of) knowledge, this marks an important difference from human belief acquisition. In our case, the very manner in which we form our beliefs, unlike non-human animals, does change over time. More than this, the manner in which our

[40] 'Knowledge and Intellectual Virtue', repr. in *Knowledge in Perspective: Selected Essays in Epistemology* (Cambridge University Press, 1991), 240.

[41] 'Is Knowledge a Natural Phenomenon?', in R. Schantz (ed.), *The Externalist Challenge* (de Gruyter, 2004), 209.

processes of belief acquisition and revision are modified over time is intimately connected both to reflection and to agency. We human beings periodically stop to reflect on our own beliefs and the manner in which they are acquired and revised, as well as on our own past track record of success and failure. At times, we take steps self-consciously to modify the ways in which we arrive at and revise our beliefs. Thus, for example, when students in an introductory logic class discover that they have been regularly affirming the consequent, and that this inferential strategy is wildly unreliable, at least some of them try to train themselves to stop affirming the consequent; that is, they try to break themselves of a bad inferential habit. This kind of cognitive self-management, it seems, is unique to human beings, and it is a power we have as a result of our ability to reflect on our own mental states.

The suggestion, then, is that reflection allows us to engage in cognitive self-management, unlike other animals, and our ability to monitor our own cognition, and to actively retrain ourselves so as to more accurately form beliefs lends a dimension to our cognition which other animals lack. By the time human beings are adults—and, indeed, arguably well before that—the manner in which we arrive at our beliefs can no longer be accounted for by the direct operation of our native inferential processes. Rather, our (admittedly periodic) scrutiny of our own cognitive performance prompts self-conscious action aimed at cognitive retraining. Many of the processes of belief acquisition and revision in any given adult will thus be the direct result of such active self-modification, just as many of the habitual actions which any adult performs are due to self-conscious activities designed to bring about the habits which produced them. More than this, even in the case of the very many processes of belief acquisition which are not the product of such self-conscious modification, their continued presence in us is explained, in part, by the fact that they have survived our periodic self-scrutiny. It is for this reason that we may reasonably think, it seems, that even unreflective human belief acquisition is importantly different from animal cognition. Even when we fail to reflect, the ways in which we arrive at our beliefs are to be explained, at least in part, by the activities which were prompted when we reflected in the past.

It is for this reason, as well, that we may reasonably be held responsible for the beliefs we hold, unlike non-human animals, and also why, unlike non-human animals, we may be said to deserve credit for our beliefs when they are arrived at reliably. It is not that our beliefs themselves are freely chosen. We do not freely choose our beliefs even when we reflect on what it is that we should believe. Rather, we, unlike other animals, may form our beliefs in ways which are influenced by our self-consciously chosen actions, and thus, we may be credited with a kind of epistemic agency which they lack. When mature human beings arrive at their beliefs in reliable ways, the cognitive mechanisms which produce and retain their beliefs are thus reasonably seen as virtues: not just mechanisms built in by the action of natural selection, but mechanisms whose very presence is due to active intervention by way of self-conscious activity prompted by reflection.[42]

Attractive and commonsensical as this picture is, I believe that it is deeply mistaken about both human and animal cognition. It underestimates the sophistication of animal cognition, and presents an account of the human case which is overly intellectualized. It presents reflection as more deeply involved in our cognition than it really is, and it gives an account of the role of agency in cognition which ties it more closely to reflection than our current understanding of the facts can support. Each of these points requires discussion and elaboration.

First, on the picture just presented, the mechanisms by which humans arrive at and revise their beliefs change over time, while, in the animal case, they do not. But the problem with this suggestion, as we have already seen, is that it is simply untrue. Many non-human animals are quite sophisticated cognitively, and the manner in which they acquire beliefs changes over time in response to new information, just as it does in human beings. Changes of this sort do not require self-conscious reflection. Beliefs, both human and non-human, may change as a result of exposure to new information, even without the intervention of self-conscious reflection. Thus, for example, as soon as I see my car keys on the kitchen table, I come to believe that they are there even if I had believed that I left them in the dining room prior to seeing them in the kitchen. This does not require reflecting on my earlier belief, or my newly acquired sense

---

[42] There are certainly many points of contact between this view and Sosa's. As mentioned above, Sosa does, at least at times, stress the importance of the distinction between human belief—whether reflectively arrived at or unreflectively arrived at—and the beliefs of non-human animals, rather than the distinction between reflectively arrived at belief and unreflectively arrived at belief. He does, in addition, focus a good deal of attention on the suggestion that we deserve credit for beliefs aptly formed (although without connecting this to self-scrutiny in the way suggested here).

experience, or the way in which my new sense experience should be integrated into my total body of beliefs. I see the keys on the table and my cognitive machinery does the work of updating my beliefs without any reflection or activity on my part.[43] The same is true in the non-human case. My dog eats his food and fully recognizes when his food dish is emptied. If after arriving at the belief that his dish is empty, he finds that I have refilled the dish, his belief about the contents of the dish are updated by his cognitive mechanisms, without any need for reflection or activity of any sort.

But just as beliefs, both human and non-human, may be updated without the need for reflection or activity, the manner in which beliefs are arrived at may be updated and revised without the need for reflection or activity. If whenever I see a fox approach, I come to believe that it is dangerous, the discovery that a particular fox is harmless will not be something that I simply register atomistically; it will bring about a change in the inferences I draw when I am confronted with this particular fox— assuming, of course, that I can recognize it when I see it again. But the same sort of inferential integration, and change in inferential tendencies, can be found in many non-human animals, as we have already noted. One needn't have anything like the cognitive sophistication of a primate, let alone a human being, in order to integrate information in this sort of way.[44] The suggestion that this ability is a by-product of the ability to reflect, and thus, unique to human beings, is mistaken.

It is important to note that this error misrepresents cognition in both humans and non-human animals. It presents non-human animals as incapable of integrating new information in ways which will inform their subsequent information processing. And it presents human beings as having the ability to integrate new information in this way only by virtue of their ability to reflect on their own mental states. Both of these claims are incorrect. But these are not the only problems with the proposed view.

Reflection is presented, on the proposed picture, as the driving agent of cognitive improvement. According to this view, when we reflect on our

---

[43] Sosa, at times, suggests that the integration of new information, at least when there are considerations at work which might individually pull in more than one direction, requires reflection on the content of one's beliefs and their logical relations, thereby making it a uniquely human possibility. This is similar to the suggestion made by Sydney Shoemaker which was examined in Ch. 2.

[44] Alcock, *Animal Behavior: An Evolutionary Approach*, is particularly instructive here.

beliefs and how they came about, on their logical relations to one another, and on our own past cognitive successes and failures, we come to initiate actions which will allow us to arrive at beliefs more accurately in the future. I have no doubt that we do, indeed, sometimes behave in just this way, and that this sort of behavior is something which no other animal can engage in. This is the important grain of truth in the suggested view. But the importance of this point is greatly exaggerated on this picture. We have already seen that animals incapable of reflection may integrate new information they obtain in ways that change the manner in which they process information. So we should not think that the highly sophisticated reflective strategy available to humans is the only manner in which cognitive improvement may come about. Non-human animals are not doomed to repeat the same cognitive errors throughout their lives simply in virtue of their inability to reflect on their mental states.

Even apart from this point, however, we have also seen that reflecting on our beliefs is not nearly so efficacious in producing cognitive improvement as the commonsense picture would have us believe. The act of reflection is often epiphenomenal with respect to the fixation of belief.[45] Here, as in many other things, phenomenology is a terribly inaccurate guide to the workings of the mind.

Because of these distortions in self-understanding, the commonsense picture of the extent of our influence over the ways in which we process information grossly exaggerates our own efficacy.[46] Thus, it is simply untrue that, as the story we are considering suggests, by the time we are adults, the processes by which we arrive at our beliefs are all either a product of actions self-consciously undertaken with the goal of improving our cognition, or, alternatively, processes which have been left as they were found under reflection only because they passed muster when they were self-consciously scrutinized. A great many cognitive processes are

---

[45] See Alison Gopnik, 'How we Know our Minds: The Illusion of First-Person Knowledge of Intentionality', *Behavioral and Brain Sciences*, 16 (1993), 1–15 and 90–101, and the discussion in section 1.3 above.

[46] This is part and parcel of the way in which the commonsense picture exaggerates our own efficacy across the board. See e.g. Shelley Taylor and Jonathan Brown, 'Illusion and Well-Being: A Social Psychological Perspective on Mental Health', *Psychological Bulletin*, 103 (1988), 193–210, and Shelly Taylor, *Positive Illusions: Creative Self-Deception and the Healthy Mind* (Basic Books, 1989).

informationally encapsulated in cognitive modules.[47] The workings of these cognitive modules will inevitably contravene the commonsense picture in two different ways: the operations of these modules are invisible to introspection, so they can never be scrutinized by reflection in the manner proposed; and, in addition, the mechanisms by which they work are simply hard-wired, so any defect that the reflective mind might detect in them would be immune to change in any case. It is, of course, a good thing that we are endowed with many cognitive processes which have these features. Our ability to respond both quickly and reliably to much of the complex character of the environment is deeply dependent on the workings of such processes. But this is just to say that the commonsense picture, which presents the workings of our own minds as very much a product of our own activity, grossly mischaracterizes the extent to which our cognitive operations are genuinely malleable. Natural selection has organized the mind in such a way as to make many of its most important features tamper-proof: they cannot be restructured by the action of a well-meaning but frequently uninformed or misinformed agent. The mind doesn't work the way the commonsense picture portrays it, and it's a good thing that it doesn't.

The attempt to portray our cognitive successes as, one and all, a product of the actions and endorsements which flow from our own reflective self-scrutiny gives us far more credit for the workings of our minds than we deserve.[48] This puts an end, I believe, to any project which would view us as deserving credit whenever we have beliefs which are aptly formed, or would see our intellectual capacities as virtues, whose very presence is to be explained by our acts of intellectual self-cultivation.[49]

---

[47] The classic presentation of this account may be found in Jerry Fodor, *The Modularity of Mind* (MIT Press, 1983).

[48] A similar point is made by Jennifer Lackey in 'Why we Don't Deserve Credit for Everything we Know', *Synthese*, 158 (2007), 345–61.

[49] By the same token, those who present pictures of the self as 'self-constituting' (see especially Christine Korsgaard's *The Sources of Normativity*; *The Constitution of Agency: Essays on Practical Reason and Moral Psychology* (Oxford University Press, 2008); and *Self-Constitution: Agency, Identity, and Integrity* (Oxford University Press, 2009); and, for a similar idea, Robert Kane, *The Significance of Free Will* (Oxford University Press, 1996)) exaggerate the role of reflective acts of character building and creation in determining the nature of the self.

3.8 Conclusion

The view that freedom of the will requires some sort of higher-order critical assessment of one's first-order states leads to an infinite regress. As we have seen, however, the regress problem is not the only difficulty with such a view. The attempt to vet one's first-order states by way of reflective higher-order review presupposes a kind of default legitimacy for higher-order states which they simply do not have. There is a certain irony here. The move to critical assessment of first-order states is motivated by the recognition that one's first-order desires, for example, may fail to reflect one's true self; they may, in an important sense, be alien influences. But the same point applies equally to higher-order states, and so we cannot distinguish between desires which are truly our own and those which are alien influences by looking to see which first-order states are backed by second-order endorsements. Second-order states, like their first-order cousins, are not self-legitimating. The problems with the view that free-dom of the will requires higher-order endorsement mirrors the problems detailed in previous chapters for similar views about knowledge and reasoning.

We next turned to an examination of a special case of agency. A very wide range of philosophers have presented views of belief acquisition which appeal to some notion of epistemic agency. These authors do not typically endorse the view that belief acquisition is a voluntary activity, and so the appeal to agency of any sort here is prima facie puzzling. Several different motivations for taking talk of epistemic agency seriously were examined, and in each of these cases, appeals to reflection and the higher-order states it produces play a crucial role. Here too, however, we saw that these views presuppose a variety of empirical claims about reflection and higher-order states which run counter to our best available evidence. If there is any legitimate notion of epistemic agency, it cannot do the work which these authors require of it.

4

Normativity

Human beings acquire beliefs and perform actions. Some of the beliefs we acquire, however, are ones we should not acquire, and some of the actions we perform are ones we should not perform. In a word, we are subject to normative demands. What is the source of these normative demands, and how is it that they can have dominion over us?

On its face, any sort of realist view about normative demands seems implausible. Normative demands do not seem to be part of the furniture of the world, something 'out there' which we might encounter, in the way that we encounter tables and chairs, other people, or microphysical objects. The idea that there might be normative demands which have dominion over us is not simply some sort of causal fact, in the way that it is a simple causal fact about the world that the laws of physics have a kind of dominion over us and that we are subject to their constraints. We can, and sometimes do, violate normative requirements. We do not ever, nor is it possible to, violate the laws of physics.

But if normative demands are not part of the furniture of the world, something 'out there' which we encounter, where precisely do they come from and how is it that they have whatever power that they do over us? One natural thought is that they come from within, that their source is not external to us, but in ourselves. More than this, it is a certain distinctive feature of human beings which seems to be the source of normativity, and which provides an explanation of the kind of power which normative demands can make on our beliefs and our actions. It is, in particular, our ability to reflect on our beliefs and actions—something non-human animals cannot do—which explains the source and power of normativity.

We do not hold non-human animals responsible for their behavior or their beliefs, and, in this respect, we treat them differently from other human beings. Non-human animals may be designed by the forces of natural selection in a way which allows them to arrive at beliefs reliably, but when they do so, they do not deserve any credit for their achievement. By the same token, when natural selection instills various processes of belief acquisition which are unreliable, and which regularly produce false beliefs, non-human animals do not seem deserving of blame. They are the unwitting beneficiaries, and the unwitting victims, of natural forces which are beyond their control. And the same is true of non-human animal behavior. Non-human animals may behave in ways which have extremely beneficial consequences, or, at times, just the reverse, but they deserve neither credit nor blame for their actions. And, in this respect, they seem quite different from human beings. Why should this be so?

The difference, it seems, lies in our greater cognitive sophistication. Non-human animals form beliefs on the basis of other beliefs they have, and they act in ways which are informed by their beliefs and desires. But we do not automatically acquire beliefs or engage in action when our first-order beliefs and desires provide such a rationale. We are capable of reflecting on our beliefs and desires, stopping to assess them, and stopping to question the wisdom and the advisability of further belief or action. When we reflect, and when we engage in reflective evaluation of our first-order states, it seems that we bring to bear certain normative standards on our beliefs and actions in a way that other animals could not possibly do. But if the norms which govern beliefs and action are not to be found outside of us, and reflection is thus not to be credited with the simple discovery of these independently existing norms, then perhaps reflection is instead to be credited with the creation of norms which bind us. Indeed, if the norms are somehow internal to us, products of our own reflective activity, then it seems that this very fact about them might serve, in part, to explain how it is that they may have the power that they do over our thought and action.

In this chapter, we will examine views which locate the source of normativity in our ability to reflect on our first-order beliefs, desires, and actions.

4.1 The infinite regress

Let us return to a passage from Christine Korsgaard, part of which we quoted earlier, for it bears additional scrutiny.

A lower animal's attention is fixed on the world. Its perceptions are its beliefs and its desires are its will. It is engaged in conscious activities, but it is not conscious *of* them. That is, they are not the objects of its attention. But we human animals turn our attention on to our perceptions and desires themselves, on to our own mental activities, and we are conscious *of* them. That is why we can think *about* them.

And this sets us a problem no other animal has. It is the problem of the normative. For our capacity to turn our attention on to our own mental activity is also a capacity to distance ourselves from them, and to call them into question. I perceive, and I find myself with a powerful impulse to believe. But I back up and bring that impulse into view and then I have a certain distance. Now the impulse doesn't dominate me and now I have a problem. Shall I believe? Is this perception really a *reason* to believe? I desire and I find myself with a powerful impulse to act. But I back up and bring that impulse into view and then I have a certain distance. Now the impulse doesn't dominate me and now I have a problem. Shall I act? Is this desire really a *reason* to act? The reflective mind cannot settle for perception and desire, not just as such. It needs a *reason*. Otherwise, at least as long as it reflects, it cannot commit itself or go forward.

If the problem springs from reflection then the solution must do so as well. If the problem is that our perceptions and desires might not withstand reflective scrutiny, then the solution is that they might. We need reasons because our impulses must be able to withstand reflective scrutiny. We have reasons if they do. The normative word 'reason' refers to a kind of reflective success.[1]

What Korsgaard suggests here is that there is a very tight connection between reflection and correct normative standards. Having reasons, on this view, whether for belief or for action, just is a matter of having a certain sort of reflective success. What it is for a belief or action to meet appropriate normative standards is nothing more nor less than that it survive reflective scrutiny.

So let us consider the case of belief which Korsgaard describes. I find myself with a strong inclination to believe a certain proposition, and I stop and reflect: I wonder whether I really ought to believe it. This, as Korsgaard rightly says, presents me with a problem. Now suppose I subject this belief to critical scrutiny and I find that it passes my standards; it meets with a certain reflective success. Does this mean that I ought to believe this particular proposition? Does it mean that I have reason to believe it?

It is quite clear that the answer to these two questions need not be 'yes'. It may be that the standards I bring to bear when I reflect are not very good ones. As we saw in section 1.3, when individuals reflect on their beliefs, the process of reflection may do little more than serve to ratify whatever belief is being considered. The normative question about what I ought to

[1] Korsgaard, *The Sources of Normativity* (Cambridge University Press, 1996), 92–3.

believe, and what I have reason to believe, is not a question about whether the proposed belief passes my standards, whatever those standards may be. I might reasonably wonder whether the standards I have are good ones or reasonable ones; whether passing my standards gives me any reason at all to think that the proposed belief is true. The concern which the reflective agent has does not seem to be a concern about whether his or her belief would be reflectively endorsed, for we are all familiar with cases in which an agent stops to reflect on one of his beliefs, finds that it passes his own benighted standards, and goes on holding the belief in a far more self-confident, but no less misguided way. The reflective epistemic agent is concerned to have beliefs which are true, and what he is looking for is reasons to believe that the belief in question is true or is likely to be true. Passing reflective scrutiny may sometimes provide us with reasons, if the standards we reflectively apply are good ones; but passing reflective scrutiny cannot be identified with having a reason regardless of the standards applied.

Just as first-order beliefs are not automatically rational, second-order beliefs about what one ought to believe or do are not automatically rational. And this just means that when one reflectively endorses a particular belief, one may still have no reason at all to believe it.[2]

Now no one believes that having a reason is to be identified with reflective endorsement regardless of how that endorsement is achieved; certainly Korsgaard doesn't believe this. The process of reflective scrutiny may, for example, be performed too casually or broken off too soon. For example, in the case of moral reasons, Korsgaard comments:

Kantian positions in general set a high value on reflection and are idealizing positions in the sense that moral concepts, as Kant defines them, are derived from the ideal of a fully reflective person. The fully reflective person is a corollary of Kant's idea of the unconditioned. We seek the unconditioned by imagining a person who reasons all the way back, who never gives up until there is a completely

---

[2] Even the most ardent internalist should believe this. To believe otherwise is either to give second-order beliefs an epistemic free-ride which one denies to first-order beliefs, or to endorse an unreasonable form of conservatism which allows that the mere fact of believing something, however otherwise unreasonable that belief may be, provides one with a reason to go on believing it. For an important and, to my mind, completely persuasive argument against the latter, see David Christensen, 'Conservatism in Epistemology', *Noûs*, 28 (1994), 69–89. Even those who endorse conservatism should still reject Korsgaard's view, however, for the very weak reasons which conservatism provides, on such views, may easily be outweighed by other reasons.

undeniable, satisfying, unconditional answer to the question. Obviously human beings often stop reflecting very far short of that.[3]

So the crucial question here is just what it means to 'reason all the way back', and what it means to reach a result that is, as Korsgaard suggests, 'completely undeniable'. It is not at all obvious what this could be.

So let us take a concrete example. Suppose I believe that the President is doing an excellent job of managing political debate on a controversial policy, and that he will soon be able to get his favored legislation passed by Congress. I stop to reflect on this belief, and I ask myself whether I really have good reason to believe this. As soon as I raise this question, a number of points immediately come to mind. My belief that the President is doing a fine job of managing the debate is hardly uncontroversial. Not only his political opponents, but many of his political supporters as well, have recently doubted whether the President has the situation under control. And I recognize as well that I am such a staunch supporter of the President, and I so badly want this particular piece of legislation to pass Congress, that my belief about the President's control over the current situation could, perhaps, be a product of wishful thinking rather than just my sensitivity to reasons for belief. So I need to be especially careful in reflecting upon my reasons.

When I reflect upon my reasons for believing that the President will be successful in getting his legislation passed by Congress, the reasons I have for that belief seem to be good ones. But surely this alone cannot constitute reasoning 'all the way back'. I am aware that reflection can be too casual, and I am aware, as well, that reflection itself, just like first-order reasoning, can be biased and unreliable. So I wonder whether my reflective (second-order) assessment of my first-order reasons should be taken at face value. And this requires some sort of third-order assessment, which itself cannot be taken at face value. So the idea that we must scrutinize our reasons 'all the way back' inevitably leads to an infinite regress.

Any time we stop scrutinizing our reasons and settle for our n^{th}-order assessment of them, we leave some of our reasons unscrutinized and thereby leave open the possibility that these reasons themselves, and all the other reasons at lower levels which they endorse as legitimate, are themselves

---

[3] This passage occurs in an interview with Korsgaard: 'Christine M. Korsgaard: Internalism and the Sources of Normativity', in Herlinde Pauer-Studer (ed.), *Constructions of Practical Reason: Interviews on Moral and Political Philosophy* (Stanford University Press, 2002), 60.

illegitimate. In light of the psychological evidence discussed earlier, this kind of worry is not remotely pathological. If what were needed to solve this problem were an ability to reason 'all the way back', an ability to arrive at a result which provides 'a completely undeniable, satisfying, unconditional answer to the question' one is trying to resolve, then it should be perfectly clear that such a solution is simply impossible, and that a solution to the normative questions we wish to ask is hopelessly out of our reach.

4.2 The perfectibility of human reason

The real problem with Korsgaard's suggestion here, however, is not that it leads to an infinite regress. Even if we were, *per impossibile*, able to reason 'all the way back', the normative standards we would thereby apply need not tell us anything about the normative status of our beliefs or actions. The problem here is that Korsgaard has misunderstood what the normative problem is.

Checking one's first-order beliefs by way of second-order reflection may be problematic because the biases and simple unreliability of first-order processes may come into play at the second-order as well. In general, problems at any given level of reflection may be reintroduced when one moves one level up. But the solution to this problem cannot be simply to reflect longer and deeper, for this is a problem about reflection generally. Reflection is not automatically more reliable than the processes of belief acquisition it is recruited to scrutinize, and, in actual practice, reflecting on lower-level beliefs and inclinations to action often fails to identify the very problems it is intended to correct. We thus cannot simply identify proper normative standards with those which survive reflective scrutiny, even if it were carried on indefinitely long. We know all too well that reflective scrutiny, however carefully, thoughtfully, and lengthily engaged in, can, and often does, mislead us about normative concerns.

As Korsgaard sees it, the normative problem is one about reflective scrutiny. 'If the problem is that our perceptions and desires might not withstand reflective scrutiny,' she remarks, 'then the solution is that they might.' But the normative problem is not that our perceptions and desires might not withstand reflective examination. The normative worry I have about my belief that the President's policy will be passed by Congress is not that it might not pass my reflective standards. I am not looking for consolation that, whatever my standards may be, this belief meets those standards. I have seen others whose beliefs met their standards, and I recognize that these cases fall into two importantly different classes: those whose standards are normatively appropriate and those whose standards are not. Knowing that, if my belief meets my standards, I fall into one of these two classes, provides me with no consolation at all. I want my beliefs to be true, and, for that very reason, I want the processes which produce them to be reliable. I want my beliefs to be responsive to reasons. Since meeting my reflective standards, however far back those standards are scrutinized, need not be a good indicator of whether my belief is true or reliably produced or responsive to reasons, it would be a mistake to see meeting my reflective standards as my real goal here. At best, reflecting on whether my beliefs and actions meet my standards might be instrumental to achieving my goal of having beliefs and actions which are properly responsive to reason. Clearly, unless my processes of reflection are themselves responsive to reason, no amount of reflective checking on my beliefs and actions is going to be helpful here. But no amount of reflective checking can address that issue.

The problem here is not one of circularity. It is, instead, a problem raised by the simple fact that reflection is not automatically more reliable than the processes it is recruited to check on. Once we see this, the question of the reliability of reflection becomes crucial, and, as we have seen, there is a good deal of research on this very issue. It does not support reliance on reflection for identifying problems with lower level processes. Far from determining normative standards, unaided reflection does not even reliably discover them.

In his first inaugural address, Bill Clinton offered an extremely optimistic view of the United States: 'There is nothing wrong with America that can't be cured by what is right with America.' A similar view about human reason seems to underlie Korsgaard's account of reflective endorsement. Human beings are susceptible to certain sorts of bad reasoning. At the same time, we are able to discover that some of the reasoning to which we are prone is bad, and we do this, at least in part, by reflecting on the character of our reasoning. So what is good in our reasoning seems to work to correct what is bad. If we were to continue this process, 'all the way back', would we end up with proper reasoning? That is certainly one possibility. But it is an empirical bet, and a highly controversial one at that. Even if reason were perfectible in this way, it is one thing to suggest that we are fortunate enough to be natively endowed with basic processes of reasoning which are good enough so that turning them back on themselves will result in an understanding of proper principles of reasoning; it is quite another thing to *identify* good reasoning with the outcome of such a process. Even on the extremely optimistic view that human reason would fully correct itself, it would be a mistake simply to identify good reasoning a priori with whatever might be the outcome of the self-reflective process. But without any such additional assumption, the suggestion that even an idealized reflective endorsement serves to provide us with an account of reason, or the source of normativity, is entirely unmotivated.

What are we to suppose would happen should we turn reflective and try to determine what it is that we ought to believe? Let us return to the case of my belief that the President will be able to get his favored piece of legislation passed by Congress. When I reflect on this belief and try to determine whether I really ought to hold it, a number of issues immediately come to the fore. I need to reflect on my other beliefs to see whether they genuinely provide support for this controversial claim. I also need to consider my views about what it is that constitutes adequate evidence for belief. Finally, I need to consider a host of psychological claims about myself: questions about the reliability of my memory; my susceptibility to wishful thinking; the extent to which I have thoroughly and evenhandedly gone about the task of evidence gathering. Unless I consider all of these issues, I cannot claim to arrive at a determination of what it is that I ought to believe which will fully withstand reflective scrutiny.

Let us consider the psychological issues first. If I am genuinely interested in finding out the answers to the relevant psychological questions, it is perfectly clear that unaided reflection is ill-suited to resolving these issues. If one wants to know whether one's memory is reliable, it simply won't do just to reflect on that question to see whether it seems to be so. If one wants to know whether one is the sort of person who regularly engages in wishful thinking, merely reflecting on the question is not a terribly effective way to find an accurate answer. And if one wants to know whether one has pursued an inquiry in an evenhanded and unbiased manner, merely reflecting and asking oneself whether one has in fact met these standards is not a good way to determine whether one actually has. In all of these cases, external checks on these issues are absolutely essential. The very mechanisms which produce biased or unreliable first-order results often act in ways that hide their workings from reflective scrutiny. And this means that any equilibrium reached by unaided reflection may amount to nothing more than a foolish consistency. But without an answer to these psychological questions, one is in no position to determine what one ought to believe, even if one knew exactly what one's other beliefs were, and even if one had a complete and accurate answer to the question of what it is that makes for adequate evidence for belief.

The question of what my other beliefs are, of course, raises similar issues. This is a psychological question, and reflection is not well-suited to fully and accurately answer it. When I reflect, no doubt I come to form views about what my other beliefs are. In the case at hand, I come to form beliefs about what other beliefs I have which are relevant to the question at issue. Even leaving aside, for a moment, questions about the accuracy of my beliefs about what other beliefs I hold, one should have real doubts about the extent to which one can get at all of the beliefs one holds which bear on the question at issue. For any complicated issue, such as the one about the President's favored legislation, there is an extraordinarily wide range of one's beliefs which bear on it. When one responds to queries from others about why one holds such a belief, one inevitably gives only a partial accounting of the relevant evidence in one's possession. Giving a full accounting, even to oneself, is surely an extremely difficult task. If one's view of evidence is holistic, this would require providing oneself with an inventory of all of one's beliefs, surely an impossible task. Even if one holds a view about evidence which is less holistic, cases like this one which involve inference to an explanation surely involve a very wide range of evidence, evidence which one may be sensitive to even without being able to give any fully explicit accounting of it. But in order to reach the kind of stable equilibrium which Korsgaard has in mind here, a full accounting of all of one's evidence must be given so that it can be laid bare to reflective scrutiny. It would be unreasonable to think that this is something which anyone can do.

Finally, there is the question of the proper relationship between evidence and theory. Here, at last, it may seem, is an issue which is independent of the kinds of psychological issues we have just been considering. The proper relationship between evidence and theory, on at least some views, can be addressed by reason alone. It would be a mistake, however, to think that psychological issues do not come into play here. Just as my views about various political matters may be influenced by bias, wishful thinking, or simple unreliability, the same is true of matters of 'pure reason'. When it comes to various claims about the proper relationship between evidence and theory, these issues are matters of intense philosophical controversy, and it would be foolish to think that one's views on these matters could not be influenced by idiosyncracies of one's philosophical training, one's professional allegiances, wishful thinking, indeed, all of the psychological factors that come into play when we leave the realm of 'pure reason'.[4] So there is no hope, even here, of leaving psychological matters out of the picture. Any equilibrium we reach will need to involve views about our own psychology, and it would be irresponsible to arrive at such views by way of reflection alone.

These points about the relevance of psychological factors, and the impossibility of responsibly and accurately arriving at views about what one should believe without taking such issues into account, are not meant merely to show something about the epistemology of normative questions. It is, beyond doubt, important to point out that substantive psychological questions are always relevant to any inquiry whatever, but Korsgaard wishes to make a claim not about the epistemology of normative claims, but, instead, the metaphysics of such claims. What she is arguing is that the truth-makers for claims about what one ought to believe are nothing more than certain facts about what one would believe upon reflection alone. But what one would believe on reflection alone, in the absence of relevant background information about one's own psychology, need not accurately reflect, let alone constitute, the truth about normativity.[5]

I have been supposing that Korsgaard's attempt to identify normative truths with the stable results of normative reflection should be understood as involving reflection on one's current state, a kind of inquiry in which

---

[4] Jerry Cohen nicely illustrates this point in some personal reminiscences in the title essay of *If You're an Egalitarian, How Come You're So Rich?* (Harvard University Press, 2001).

[5] Indeed, it is not at all clear that there is some unique answer to the claim of what one would believe about these matters on reflection, and thus, one implication of this view might well be a certain sort of relativism about normative matters. How disturbing such a relativistic view would be would depend, to my mind, on the range of views one might stably reach on reflection. I see no reason to think that the scope of such a relativism would be narrowly constrained. Order effects would likely play a non-trivial role in determining the equilibrium which would be reached (assuming that any equilibrium at all is possible). This doesn't, to my mind, look at all like the sort of thing which could constitute the truth (or the truths) about normative matters.

one stands back from one's beliefs and desires and takes reflective stock of where one stands. Such an inquiry may, to be sure, take a good deal of time, but it is an inquiry which does not involve additional empirical investigation; it is conducted using the powers of reflection alone. Certainly this is what the passages I've quoted from Korsgaard seem to suggest. There is, however, another way in which one might understand the suggestion that normative truths are to be identified with the stable results of normative reflection, one which requires that the stability achieved should pass a more stringent test.

We have seen that normative reflections on one's beliefs and desires need not converge to normative truths, even if a stable equilibrium is reached, because one's reflections themselves may proceed in a way which is biased, misguided, or simply unreliable. One might perhaps think, however, that any such mistaken equilibrium would be likely to prove unstable in the face of further empirical inquiry. Normative truths might thus be identified with the stable results of reflective normative inquiry, not by standing back from one's beliefs and desires at an instant and reflecting on normative questions without further empirical input, but by engaging in normative reflection with the aid of further empirical input. The normative results one reaches must thus withstand not only reflection on one's current state, but they must remain stable even in the face of further engagement with the world. This is not, quite clearly, what Korsgaard has in mind, but it is, nevertheless, a suggestion worth considering.

It should be clear, however, that even this more stringent requirement will not guarantee convergence of any kind, let alone convergence on normative truths. Empirical inquiry may turn up misleading evidence of various sorts, and so it need not inform, but may instead distort, the results it produces. The idea that empirical investigation is likely to correct mistakes which might otherwise result is overly optimistic; whether it is likely to produce such beneficial results is very much dependent on the kinds of questions which are being addressed, the circumstances in which the investigation is carried out, and the background beliefs and cognitive capacities of the investigator who conducts the inquiry. The idea that such an investigation must inevitably correct any errors is clearly just mistaken. Neither second-order processes, such as reflection, nor the first-order processes which are involved in ordinary empirical inquiry, nor any combination of the two are such that their outcomes may simply be identified with truths of any sort. Normative truths are no exception.

The idea of insulating reflection from empirical inquiry in order to locate normative truths opens the results of such reflection to a variety of different errors. Normative truths cannot be identified with the results of such a reflective inquiry. Nor can we identify normative truths with the results of such a reflective inquiry vetted by ordinary empirical means. The very idea that there is some intimate, perhaps constitutive, connection between reflection and normative truths is one which requires further scrutiny.

4.3 Normativity, prescriptivity, and the a priori

We began this chapter with a number of commonsensical claims about the normative. Normative truths (if this is even the right way to think about normative claims which are correct) are not claims about the physical world; they are not claims about something 'out there'. In addition, the kind of dominion which normative claims may have over us is different in kind from the kind of dominion which physical laws have over us. We were led, somehow, from these commonsensical thoughts to the idea that there is an important connection between normativity and reflection. We need to re-examine how it is that we arrived at such a suggestion.

There are, I believe, two importantly different routes to the idea that there is a close connection between normativity and reflection. For those who wish to endorse the claim that there is such a connection, the fact that two different routes seem to lead to the same place surely counts strongly in favor of this idea. While these two different routes have not always been clearly separated from one another, it will be important, I believe, to examine them separately.

The first route derives from a contrast between descriptive and prescriptive claims. The sciences, it seems, seek to describe the world accurately. Empirical investigation, when properly carried out, allows us to determine what the world is like; it allows us to arrive at an accurate description of the various objects, events, and processes which the world contains. Normative claims, however, are not descriptions; they are, instead, prescriptions. They do not attempt to tell us what the world is like, but, instead, how the world ought to be. This is not the sort of thing which empirical investigation could possibly reveal, since the outcome of empirical investigation, properly carried out, is nothing more than an accurate description of the world. So if we wish to discover normative truths—again, assuming that this is the right way to characterize correct normative claims—we will need to turn away from empirical methods and engage, instead, in reflection. Instead of looking outward, at the world, we will need to look inward. The idea here is an epistemological one: empirical methods provide us with access to descriptive features of the world. Our access to the normative must be by some other means, namely, by reflection. This is the thought behind the idea that normative claims can be known a priori.

There is also, however, a second kind of contrast between the descriptive and the prescriptive which seems to lead to the idea that there is close connection between normativity and reflection. While descriptive claims tell us how the world is, prescriptive claims tell us what to do or what to think. But the world can't tell us what to do or what to think. Prescription requires an agent to do the prescribing. When we turn our thoughts outward to the world and engage in empirical investigation, all we can end up with are views about how things actually stand in the world. But when we reflect, we can give ourselves prescriptions about how to behave or what to believe. Normativity involves laws of a certain sort, and the sort of laws involved here—unlike the laws of the physical sciences—require a law giver. The law giver is to be found inside us, through reflection, not out in the world. We ourselves are the source of normative laws, and it is the fact that these laws issue from us which explains why we are bound by them. It is in our role as self-legislating agents that normativity is to be found, and it is the reflective self which is the source of the commands which we give ourselves. The idea here is not an epistemological one, but a metaphysical one: while agents are the sort of thing which can issue commands, the (non-agentive) world outside us is not.

Both the epistemological route and the metaphysical route to the conclusion linking normativity and reflection are to be found in a great many philosophers. Thus, consider the argument offered[6] by Gilbert Harman in *The Nature of Morality* about the relationship between moral claims and observation. Harman asks whether moral principles can 'be tested and confirmed in the way scientific principles can',[7] and he argues that it is an 'apparent fact that ethics is cut off from observation in a way that science is

---

[6] While Harman offers this argument, it is one he does not endorse.

[7] Harman, *The Nature of Morality: An Introduction to Ethics* (Oxford University Press, 1977), 3.

not'.[8] While it obvious how we would go about making observations in order to determine whether a table is three feet long or four feet long, it is not at all obvious how observations might bear on whether, to use Harman's example, it is morally permissible to cut up a single healthy person in order to use his bodily organs to save five others. Harman is interested in the relationship between moral claims and observation, but what he says here seems to apply, just as much, to other normative claims. Observation seems to be irrelevant to fundamental normative claims, but, if it is possible to have reason to believe such claims, then our reasons must derive from some other source. This is just the epistemological point made above. Although Harman does not talk about reflection *per se*, he does point out that moral claims seem to be tested by way of thought experiments, rather than observation. This seems to be the very same point made using a different bit of terminology.

More than this, once one has made the epistemological point that observation of the physical world seems to be irrelevant to the evaluation of fundamental normative claims, it is a short step to drawing some metaphysical conclusions about normativity. If normative claims were made true by certain physical features of the world, it would be utterly inexplicable why it should be that observation seems irrelevant to their evaluation. Since observation does seem irrelevant to the evaluation of normative claims, it must be that what it is that makes them true—assuming, of course, that we do not simply abandon talk of normativity entirely—is something quite independent of the physical world. Since we look inside ourselves and reflect on hypothetical examples to evaluate normative claims, rather than make observations of the physical world, it must be that what makes normative claims true is something intimately connected to the process of reflection. Harman doesn't make this argument, but the considerations he offers strongly suggest it.

Nelson Goodman's classic discussion of the method of reflective equilibrium in *Fact, Fiction, and Forecast* takes a similar turn. Goodman is interested in the justification of both inductive and deductive inference, and he gives a uniform account of the proper route to their justification.

The point is that rules and particular inferences alike are justified by being brought into agreement with one another. *A rule is amended if it yields an inference we are unwilling to accept; an inference is rejected if it violates a rule we are unwilling to amend.* The process of justification is the delicate one of making mutual adjustments between rules and accepted inferences, and in the agreement achieved lies the only justification needed for either.[9]

On Goodman's account, then, the justification of both inductive and deductive rules is achieved by way of reflection, for we need to consider not only what inferences we actually make,[10] and what inferential rules we actually endorse, but which changes we are willing to make when we find that there is a conflict between our inferential practice and our beliefs about proper inference. Here, reflection is put to epistemological work, in discovering what rules of inference are valid.

It would be a mistake, however, to see Goodman's claim here merely as one about the epistemology of proper reasoning. Goodman does not hold that the method of reflective equilibrium allows us to discover some antecedently existing fact about valid inference, a fact which is independent of the reflective process by which it is discovered. Rather, Goodman's view is that what it is for an inference to be valid just is that it would be endorsed by the method of reflective equilibrium. Thus, he remarks:

A result of such analysis is that we can stop plaguing ourselves with certain spurious questions about induction. We no longer demand an explanation for guarantees that we do not have, or seek keys to knowledge that we cannot obtain. It dawns upon us that the traditional smug insistence upon a hard-and-fast line between justifying induction and describing ordinary inductive practice distorts the problem. And we owe belated apologies to Hume. For in dealing with the question how normally accepted inductive judgments are made, he was in fact dealing with the question of inductive validity.[11]

Inductive validity, for Goodman, just is a matter of what rules would be endorsed under conditions of reflective equilibrium.

The attempt to connect normativity with reflection, however, is presented most explicitly and in greatest detail by Korsgaard. When we engage

<hr/>

[9] Goodman, *Fact, Fiction, and Forecast*, 3rd edn. (Bobbs-Merrill, 1973), 64.

[10] Realistically, a proper account of this would require far more than mere reflection. There can be little doubt that people do have views, arrived at by way of reflection, about the inferences they actually make. But psychological research on human inference has made a great many discoveries about the inferences we make which reflection alone did not reveal. If one were to carry out the Goodmanian program properly, then, a good deal more than mere reflection would be required. Nevertheless, many who sign on to the project of arriving at some sort of Goodmanian reflective equilibrium have in mind a methodology which involves reflection alone.

[11] Ibid. 64–5.

in empirical investigation, we attempt to formulate scientific explanations of the various phenomena we find in the physical world, and we should believe in the existence of all and only those entities, states, and processes which are postulated by our best available theories. Where does this leave an investigation of the status of reasons or of normativity? Scientific investigation of the physical world does not lead to the discovery of sub-atomic particles, forces, and also reasons. We don't find electrical, chemical, and also normative properties. And this very fact may lead some to the conclusion that normative properties are not real.[12] But Korsgaard rejects this conclusion.

The point here is the same as the point I made . . . against the argument that reasons are not real because we do not need them for giving scientific explanations of what people think and do. That is not, in the first instance, what we need them for, but that does not show that they are not real. We need them because our reflective nature gives us a choice about what to do. We may need to appeal to the existence of reasons in the course of an explanation of why human beings experience choice in the way that we do, and in particular, of why it seems to us that there are reasons. But that explanation will not take the form 'it seems to us that there are reasons because there really are reasons'. Instead, it will be just the sort of explanation which I am constructing here: reasons exist because we need them, and we need them because of the structure of reflective consciousness, and so on.[13]

The suggestion that 'reasons exist because we need them' is certainly puzzling. We will need to examine it in detail.

On the scientific side, the justification for positing the existence of various entities, properties and processes is fairly straightforward. We are interested in explaining some phenomenon—perhaps, to use Harman's example, the presence of a certain track in a cloud chamber—and we find that the best explanation of the phenomenon requires positing the existence of a certain entity—in this case, a particular kind of particle. We come to believe that such particles exist, and our belief is itself explained, ultimately, by the fact which makes it true: we believe that there was a particle of a certain sort in the cloud chamber precisely because there was such a particle in the cloud chamber. If positing the existence of a certain sort of particle does no explanatory work for us, then we ought not to believe that particles of that sort exist. When we are engaged in the project

---

[12] Thus e.g. see J. L. Mackie, *Ethics: Inventing Right and Wrong* (Penguin, 1977).
[13] Korsgaard, *Sources of Normativity*, 96.

of understanding the world around us, our ontological commitments should be determined by the best explanations which we are in a position to give.

Thus, to take another more homely example, if I wish to know how much money I have in my checking account, and call my bank to ask about my balance, the best explanation for the bank telling me that my balance is one hundred dollars is simply that this is, in fact, how much money I have in my account. There could be other explanations for the bank telling me this: they could be playing a joke, or they could be trying to cheat me, or they could have simply made an error. But in the absence of special reason to believe such things, the best explanation is that my bank balance is just what the bank has told me that it is. If I need considerably more money than I have in my account in order to pay my mortgage, the fact that I need more money is not a reason to believe that I have it. On the scientific side of things, needing something is not a reason to believe that one has it.

So how could it be otherwise when it comes to reasons? Korsgaard says that 'reasons exist because we need them'. And what she has in mind here is not that we are able to explain some phenomenon better by positing the existence of reasons. 'We need them because of the structure of reflective consciousness . . .' When we try to determine what we should do or what we should believe, we need reasons to proceed. And so, Korsgaard concludes, reasons exist. How could this possibly be a legitimate inference to draw?

Korsgaard makes a similar sort of inference in discussing the role that human freedom plays in deliberation.

In the same way, we do not need the concept of 'freedom' in the first instance because it is required for giving scientific explanations of what people do, but rather to describe the condition in which we find ourselves when we reflect on what we do. But that doesn't mean that I am claiming that our experience of our freedom is scientifically inexplicable. I am claiming that it is to be explained in terms of the structure of our reflective consciousness, not as the (possibly delusory) *perception* of a theoretical or metaphysical property of the self.

The Scientific World View is a description of the world which serves the purposes of explanation and prediction. When its concepts are applied correctly it tells us things that are true. But it is not a *substitute* for human life. And nothing in human life is more real than the fact that we must make our decisions and choices 'under the idea of freedom'.[14]

---

[14] Ibid. 96–7.

So, once again, we have the claim that something is needed—in this case, freedom is needed in order to make our decisions and choices—and so, Korsgaard concludes, we have it.

Now psychologists have certainly studied what goes on during deliberation, and they are certainly familiar with the fact that we deliberate 'under the idea of freedom'. In a great many cases where individuals act in ways which give them the impression that they are acting freely, and that they have control over their actions and of various phenomena, they quite clearly are not acting freely and do not have control over the phenomena they believe themselves to control. Thus, for example, Michael Frank and Crystal Smith have studied the illusion of control in children who are chronic gamblers.[15] The mere fact that pathological gamblers take themselves to act freely, the fact that they experience their gambling as a free choice, should not convince us that they are correct about this. It would clearly be a mistake to think that anyone who takes himself to be acting freely, and whose deliberations are accompanied by the impression that they are freely undertaken, is automatically correct about this. Korsgaard herself acknowledges as much: 'I am claiming that [the experience of freedom] is to be explained in terms of the structure of our reflective consciousness, not as the (possibly delusory) *perception* of a theoretical or metaphysical property of the self.' So when Korsgaard says that we have freedom because we need it, and freedom is needed to explain the structure of reflective consciousness, the kind of explanation which she has in mind is not the kind of explanation which psychologists are trying to give. Since psychologists are trying to explain what it is that actually goes on in us when we have the impression that we act freely, and since they discover (unsurprisingly) that we may have this impression even when we do not act freely, it is utterly puzzling what kind of explanatory enterprise Korsgaard takes herself to be engaged in. What kind of explanatory enterprise allows us to say that we are free in making various choices simply on the basis of our acting 'under the idea of freedom', when our best scientific explanations of behavior allow that we may confidently take ourselves to be acting freely even when we are not? How is this different from concluding that I have money in my checking account because I need it to pay the mortgage?

[15] 'Illusion of Control and Gambling in Children', *Journal of Gambling Studies*, 5 (1989), 127–36.

Korsgaard's claim that we act freely in certain situations—for example, in deliberation—and her claim that reasons for belief and action exist are meant to be insulated from any possible refutation from science. I don't mean to be endorsing the claim that scientific investigation shows that there are no such things as reasons nor the claim that such investigation shows that deliberation is never free. But the suggestion that empirical investigation is irrelevant to these claims, or rather, that there is some version of these claims to which empirical investigation is irrelevant, is difficult to defend. In the case of freedom, for example, surely work psychologists have been doing on the illusion of control is relevant to questions about freedom. As I argued in section 2.5 above in discussing questions about the existence of beliefs, the suggestion that philosophers and psychologists are simply talking about different things when they each use the word 'belief' is terribly implausible. Much the same is true about the word 'freedom', and for similar reasons. Just as in the case of the word 'belief', psychologists and philosophers who talk about 'freedom' are concerned with at least many of the same explanatory issues. While there can be little doubt that there are a number of distinct conceptions of freedom which might be at issue in any of these discussions, the suggestion that the explanatory project psychologists engage in is wholly irrelevant to that of philosophers would require a good deal of argument. And we see no such argument in Korsgaard's work. We need to know just what descriptive project is involved in describing 'the condition in which we find ourselves when we reflect on what we do' which is both different, and wholly insulated, from the descriptive project psychologists are engaged in which they would describe using the very same words. We also need to know just what explanatory project is involved in providing 'an explanation of why human beings experience choice in the way that we do' which is both different, and wholly insulated, from the explanatory project which psychologists are engaged in when they use these very words. It is not at all clear what such descriptive and explanatory projects could be.

One might be interested, for example, in the phenomenology of deliberation, choice, action, and belief acquisition and retention; one might wish to describe these events 'from the inside'. Such an enterprise needn't take account of the proper psychological description or explanation of these occurrences. Thus, for example, if I am interested in describing the phenomenology of choice, I needn't consider whether the best available account which psychologists offer of choice situations actually accords with how it seems from the inside or, instead, conflicts with it. If I'm interested in nothing more than the phenomenology of choice, then a scientific account of choice situations is simply irrelevant to my enterprise. I am able to answer questions about my phenomenal experience merely by way of reflection, and the kinds of scientific questions which psychologists address are just not relevant here.[16]

While supposing that Korsgaard is interested in nothing more than the phenomenology of choice situations (involving both belief and action) would explain why she thinks that observation and scientific theorizing are irrelevant to her enterprise, it is surely implausible to suggest that it is the phenomenology of choice which is relevant to normative questions rather than an accurate understanding of the facts of the choice situation. Thus, even if the gambling activities of some pathological gamblers seem, from the inside, to be perfect exemplars of freely chosen actions, if they are genuinely in the grip of a compulsion, despite what they themselves think, our normative assessment of their behavior needs to be sensitive to this fact. If we find, to take another example, that under hypnosis, we are able to get agents to perform all manner of actions which they would not otherwise undertake, this should surely make a difference to our normative assessment of these behaviors, even if the agents themselves undertake these actions while believing themselves to be fully free. Korsgaard insists that her enterprise involves an examination of 'the structure of our reflective consciousness' rather than 'the (possibly delusory) *perception* of a theoretical or metaphysical property of the self', but proper normative assessment of action must be based on the facts about our choice situation, not our (possibly mistaken) beliefs about those facts. This is true not only of individual cases, such as the pathological gambler or the agent who slavishly conforms to some post-hypnotic suggestion; it is true, as well, about choice situations generally. If there are features of our reflective belief acquisition, or of our choice activities, about which human beings

---

[16] Or so it seems. One might, I think, reasonably ask whether subjects' beliefs about their own phenomenology tend to be accurate—i.e. accurate about their own experience—and once one raises this issue, it is no longer at all obvious that the answer must be in the affirmative. For very useful discussion of this issue, see Eric Schwitzgebel, 'The Unreliability of Naive Introspection', *Philosophical Review*, 117 (2008), 245–73. But I will not insist on this here. Instead, I will assume, for the sake of argument, that our reflective access to our own experience is perfectly accurate. If our access to our own experience is less than perfect, as I believe to be the case, then the problems for Korsgaard's position are even greater than I suggest in the text.

are generally unaware or even mistaken, the fact that we are ignorant of such things does not make them irrelevant to a proper normative assessment of our beliefs or our actions. If Korsgaard insists that it is only how things appear to us from the inside that is relevant to her descriptive and explanatory enterprise, and thus that a scientific account of how our choices and decisions are actually produced is not relevant to her concerns, then she has made the results of her inquiry irrelevant to questions of normative assessment.

The kind of Kantian view Korsgaard favors is made plausible, I believe, by the thought that the correctness of normative claims is not to be understood on the model of correspondence with some antecedently existing and external facts. We should, instead, on this view, see the correctness of normative claims as grounded in features of the self. As Korsgaard remarks,

> Each impulse as it offers itself to the will must pass a kind of test for normativity before we can adopt it as a reason for action. But the test that it must pass is not the test of knowledge or truth. For Kant, like Hume and Williams, thinks that morality is grounded in human nature, and that moral properties are projections of human dispositions. So the test is one of reflective endorsement.[17]

But even if we allow that normativity is somehow grounded in human nature, this does not very readily lead to the claim that the proper test of normative claims is that of reflective endorsement. Just as the facts about the physical world are often quite complicated and difficult to discern, the facts about human nature are not entirely transparent to the reflective self. Even if normative properties were somehow projections of human dispositions, the beliefs we form about our own dispositions when we reflect are often mistaken. Moreover, we cannot simply eliminate the need for knowledge of the relevant dispositions or features of human nature by supposing that our reflective endorsements will somehow realize the relevant dispositions. Our actual reflective endorsements are influenced by too many factors which are clearly irrelevant to normative concerns to take them entirely at face value when we engage in normative inquiry. Without a proper understanding of how reflective evaluation actually proceeds, we cannot even begin to understand the connection between

---

[17] Korsgaard, *Sources of Normativity*, 91.

reflection and normativity. Any such understanding of the reflective process, however, will need to be achieved by way of empirical research.

Both the epistemological and the metaphysical arguments which attempt to connect normativity with reflection are thus shown to be mistaken. If this sort of view is to be defended, we will need to look elsewhere.

4.4 Normativity and self-conception

Korsgaard argues that the connection between reflection and normativity may be understood by seeing the role that one's conception of one's self plays in deliberation.

> When you deliberate, it is as if there were something over and above all of your desires, something which is *you*, and which *chooses* which desire to act on. This means that the principle or law by which you determine your actions is one that you regard as being expressive of *yourself*. To identify with such a principle or way of choosing is to be, in St. Paul's famous phrase, a law to yourself.[18]

This is, I think, quite right about the phenomenology of deliberation and choice. Of course, were one to take this literally as a view about the choice situation, it would involve a rather extravagant and utterly puzzling metaphysical view of the self. If we think of the self as something literally quite separate and apart from one's desires (and presumably, one's beliefs as well), something which decides which desire to act upon, a question naturally arises as to how such a choice could be made. If the self is merely surveying one's beliefs and desires, but has neither beliefs nor desires of its own, the very idea that it might make a choice of which desire to act upon, or any choice at all, seems incoherent.

But Korsgaard does not, it seems, commit herself to the view that there is, in fact, such a self. Rather, this is merely a description of how we think about ourselves when we deliberate.

> An agent might think of herself as a Citizen of the Kingdom of Ends. Or she might think of herself as someone's friend or lover, or as a member of a family or an ethnic group or a nation.... And how she thinks of herself will determine whether it is the law of the Kingdom of Ends, or the law of some smaller group, or the law of egoism, or the law of the wanton that will be the law that she is to herself.[19]

---

[18] Ibid. 100.   [19] Ibid. 101.

What is important here, on Korsgaard's view, is merely how one thinks of oneself, not some antecedently existing facts about the self. Thus, in particular, Korsgaard denies that what is important here is ultimately a question about what the self is actually like.

The conception of one's identity in question is not a theoretical one, a view about what as a matter of inescapable scientific fact you are. It is better understood as a description under which you value yourself, a description under which you find your life worth living and your actions to be worth undertaking. So I will call this a conception of your practical identity. Practical identity is a complex matter and for the average person there will be a jumble of such conceptions. You are a human being, a woman or a man, an adherent of a certain religion, a member of an ethnic group, a member of a certain profession, someone's lover or friend, and so on. And all of these identities give rise to reasons and obligations. Your reasons express your identity, your nature; your obligations spring from what that identity forbids.[20]

So the facts about the self are not what dictate one's obligations. Rather, it is how the self appears to us under reflection which is important, regardless of whether this conception is accurate or even coherent. It is, I think, utterly puzzling why one's view of oneself under conditions of reflection should carry such weight.

More than this, Korsgaard's own examples make the suggestion that such a view of one's self, or of one's identity, should carry any weight at all even more puzzling. As Korsgaard notes, most people embrace 'a jumble of such conceptions', and, as her examples illustrate, the conceptions people have of themselves, and which, under reflection, they take to make their lives worth living and their actions worth performing, are not all terribly ennobling. For some individuals, their self-conception as a fan of a particular sports team is, as they believe under reflection, what makes their lives worth living. For others, it is their membership in the Ku Klux Klan or the Britney Spears Fan Club. Are we really to believe that 'all of these identities give rise to reasons and obligations'? Why should we believe that?

Here is what Korsgaard says.

It is the conceptions of ourselves that are most important to us that give rise to unconditional obligations. For to violate them is to lose your integrity and so your identity, and to no longer be who you are. That is, it is to no longer be able to think of yourself under the description under which you value yourself and find your life to be worth living and your actions to be worth undertaking. It is to be for all practical purposes dead or worse than dead. When an action cannot be performed without loss of some fundamental part of one's identity, and an agent could just as well be dead, then the obligation not to do it is unconditional and complete. If reasons arise from reflective endorsement, then obligation arises from reflective *rejection*.[21]

Suppose then that Joe is a member of the Ku Klux Klan, and that his membership in the Klan is, as he sees it, what gives his life meaning. I can see how Joe's Klan membership is, as Korsgaard describes it, a fundamental part of Joe's identity. But how could this possibly give rise to any obligations at all, let alone ones which are unconditional? Given the hateful and racist purposes of the Klan, surely Joe is obligated to find some other way to make his life meaningful to himself. His Klan membership could not possibly give rise to obligations which flow from its purposes merely because Joe finds meaning in them. To suggest otherwise is make a mockery of the very idea of obligations.[22] The same, I should think, is true when someone thinks of their identity as constituted by something as trivial and insignificant as membership in the Britney Spears Fan Club.

But much as this presents a problem for Korsgaard's view of unconditional obligation, there is a more pressing problem here for the attempt to connect normativity with reflection. Korsgaard says that 'It is the conceptions of ourselves that are most important to us that give rise to unconditional obligations.' But if it is what is in fact most important to us which determines our obligations, then the connection between obligation and reflection is completely severed. What we take to be important to us when we reflect,

---

[21] Ibid. 102.

[22] Korsgaard doesn't take this kind of objection very seriously. She remarks: 'One [complication] is that some parts of our identity are easily shed, and, where they come into conflict with more fundamental parts of our identity, they should be shed. The cases I have in mind are standard: a good soldier obeys orders, but a good human being doesn't massacre the innocent.' Ibid. But one cannot so easily assume that it is one's identity as a human being rather than as a soldier which is, in the relevant sense, more fundamental here. Since Korsgaard is trying to explain normativity in terms of reflection, the question about which identity is more fundamental must be one about how these identities are viewed under reflection. Our human identity may be more fundamental normatively speaking, but this is supposed to be explained by way of the appeal to what we identify with when we reflect. And just as one may regard one's religion, or one's ethnic group, as a merely accidental feature, an accident of birth, with which one does not identify, one may similarly regard one's humanity as merely an accidental feature of birth, one which is not central to one's identity. One might, in one's reflective moments, more strongly identify with one's role as a soldier. But this is just to say that this problem cannot be so easily set aside.

the authors under discussion here fully agree. Whether I turn my head is determined by my choice, but once my head is turned in a certain direction, with my eyes open, and the lighting just so, my perceptual mechanisms will simply operate in me in ways which have nothing at all to do with the fact that I am an agent. The fact that I focus my attention, and question the relevance and probity of the evidence, thus show no more agency when I reflect than goes on in unreflective cases. Indeed, these activities not only show no more epistemic agency than goes on in unreflective cases in human beings; they show no more epistemic agency than goes on in lower animals when they form perceptual beliefs. But this is just to say that these features of reflectively formed belief do not exhibit epistemic agency at all.

So, once again, we need to ask, just where are we supposed to find the workings of our epistemic agency? As I've mentioned, there are a great many sub-personal processes at work whenever we form unreflective beliefs. But in this respect too, reflection is no different. We certainly shouldn't think that what goes on in reflection is fully and accurately represented in its phenomenology, any more than it is in unreflective belief acquisition. So when we get done focusing on various bits of evidence, and considering their relevance and probity, a host of sub-personal processes go to work eventuating in the production of a belief. How, indeed, could things possibly be any different? There is, after all, a causal explanation to be had of how it is that beliefs are formed, whether belief acquisition is reflective or unreflective. We should certainly not think that while unreflective belief acquisition takes place within a causally structured series of events, leaving no room for epistemic agency (just the workings of 'peripheral modules'), reflective belief acquisition somehow takes place somewhere outside the causally structured network of events. There is, of course, no such location. But now the appeal to epistemic agency seems to be nothing more than a bit of mythology. A demystified view of belief acquisition leaves no room for its operation.

3.5 Epistemic agency and the first-person perspective

When we look at belief acquisition, even reflective belief acquisition, from the third-person perspective, there seems to be no room for epistemic and what is in fact important to us, frequently come apart. There can be little doubt that understanding our own values is a highly non-trivial project, and mere reflection will not automatically reveal to us what it is that we value most highly. One might think that attaining some professional goal is more important than anything else, only to discover, on attaining it, that it does not give one's life the meaning that one thought it did. One might think that certain personal relationships are of relatively little value to oneself, only to discover, when they are threatened, that they are more important to one's life than one took them to be. And surely any views we have about conceptions of ourselves which, were we to violate them, would make us 'for all practical purposes dead or worse than dead' must be held quite tentatively, for failures of self-understanding on such matters are probably more common than successes. Reflection does not automatically put us in touch with such deep features of the self, assuming, for the sake of argument, that there are, for each person, self-conceptions which are valued this highly. So if Korsgaard were right that our unconditional obligations are determined by the conceptions of ourselves that are most important to us, there would be no connection between reflection and normativity at all.

It would be a mistake to try to solve this problem simply by substituting 'those conceptions which we believe, under conditions of reflection, to be most valuable to us' for the problematic phrase in Korsgaard's formulation. It is, as I've argued, quite implausible to think that our deepest concerns and commitments automatically generate obligations of any sort, but it is surely more implausible still to suppose that obligations are generated by our beliefs, under reflection, about such concerns and commitments, whether these beliefs are true or not. No one should think that false beliefs about one's own deepest commitments could possibly generate obligations. But now it becomes clear that there can be no constitutive relationship whatsoever between reflection and obligation. The norms which we would reflectively endorse, or reflectively reject, need have no connection at all to reasons for action, or belief, or obligation.

Korsgaard's project goes awry at the very first step. According to Korsgaard:

It is necessary to have *some* conception of your practical identity, for without it you cannot have reasons to act. We endorse or reject our impulses by determining whether they are consistent with the ways in which we identify ourselves.[23]

---

[23]   Ibid. 120.

But if our first-order beliefs and desires did not provide us with reasons to act and to believe, then our self-conceptions—that is, our beliefs about what matters to us—could not do so either. If beliefs and desires only provide reasons if they are endorsed at some higher level, then no beliefs and no desires—including our self-conceptions—can provide us with reasons at all. We need not have self-conceptions in order to have reasons for belief and action, and when we do have self-conceptions, the mere fact that we have them cannot be the ground of our reasons or our obligations. The attempt to ground both reasons and normativity by way of self-conceptions cannot succeed.

4.5 Conclusion

There is, to be sure, a puzzle about normativity. Normative claims do not seem to be discovered by ordinary empirical means. When we examine the physical world, we are able, if we are careful and if we are lucky, to arrive at accurate descriptions of the objects around us and their many properties. But normative claims are not descriptions; they are prescriptions. And so our ordinary ways of investigating the world around us seem powerless to provide us with the prescriptions we seek. If we cannot arrive at prescriptions for belief and conduct by way of ordinary empirical investigations of the world around us, how then are such prescriptions to be found? One natural thought here is that if they are not to be found outside us, by examining the physical world, they may perhaps be found inside us by way of reflection.

There are, however, many things wrong with this thought. As we have seen, reflection on what we ought to believe and ought to do is no more self-legitimating than are our first-order beliefs and desires. And if we insist that our reflection itself must be scrutinized and reflected upon to gain legitimacy, that we must reflect 'all the way back', then we are launched on an infinite regress. This cannot enlighten us as to the source of normativity.

When we considered the norms which govern belief acquisition, the idea that they are simply constituted by the standards which we would endorse under conditions of reflection, or the standards we would reflectively endorse which meet some sort of equilibrium condition, was shown to be mistaken. Even the suggestion that such norms would be discovered by way of reflection makes certain substantive empirical assumptions about the powers of human reasoning, empirical assumptions which, as we saw, we have no reason to believe.

Attempts to ground normative claims about action in reflection fare no better. Korsgaard argues that reasons for action and obligations to act are grounded in the self-conceptions we form when we reflect, but here too we saw that such self-conceptions are not self-legitimating. Reasons and obligations could not flow from just any self-conception which a person formed under conditions of reflection, and the very idea that our first-order states could not provide us with reasons without the backing of such self-conceptions leads to an infinite regress. If reasons and obligations required higher-order endorsements to gain legitimacy, then the having of reasons and obligations would be an impossibility.

The relationship between prescriptions and descriptions is, admittedly, a puzzling one. The puzzle here, however, does nothing at all to motivate the idea that we should look inside ourselves to find a basis for prescriptions. If looking outside ourselves could give us nothing but descriptions, then it would be hard to see how looking inside ourselves could do anything else. When we reflect, we may discover our beliefs and desires and other mental states; we may discover what it is that we identify with. But this is just to say that, like looking outward, looking inward may provide us with reasons to believe certain descriptive claims. If descriptive claims could give us no reason at all for believing normative claims, as the worry about looking out at the world presupposes, then looking inward could do no better. If this is the puzzle which prompts us to worry about the source of normativity, we should not think that its solution will be found in reflection.

5

Reflection Demystified

We have examined four related topics on which philosophers have appealed to reflection in order to solve important problems: we have looked at knowledge and justification; reasons and reasoning; freedom of the will; and normativity. In each case, a problem has been identified at the first-order level which is, allegedly, resolved by appealing to second-order states produced by reflection. There is a parallel structure to the discussion of these four topics. The need for reflection is prompted, in each case, by a commonsensical requirement which, on closer examination, leads to an infinite regress. If a belief could only be justified if it were subjected to higher-order scrutiny, then no belief could be justified. If one belief could only serve as a reason for another if it were believed to be a reason for that belief, then no belief could serve as a reason for another. If freedom of the will required higher-order scrutiny of one's beliefs and desires, then freedom of the will would be impossible. And if we could account for the source and legitimacy of normative demands only by seeing them as imposed upon us by reflection 'all the way back', then we could not account for the source or legitimacy of normative demands. Once we recognize that mental states are not automatically self-legitimizing, we must recognize that this applies not only to first-order states, but to the second-order states we arrive at by way of reflection. There is no second-order magic. Second-order mental states are not so very different from first-order mental states: both are firmly entwined in the same causal net; both are, at times, reasons-responsive and, at times, disengaged from reason. We should not think that because a mental state is second-order that it automatically solves or sidesteps the philosophical problems which arise for first-order states.

As we have seen, however, the regress problem is not the only difficulty which arises for attempts to recruit reflection to resolve philosophical difficulties. Even more modest appeals to reflection, ones which somehow evade the infinite regress, depend on an overly optimistic view about the powers of reflection. If we are worried, for example, about the reliability of first-order belief acquisition unaided by reflection because we recognize that first-order processes are not uniformly reliable, we cannot simply take for granted that the processes by which we reflect on our first-order states will improve our reliability. As we have seen, the various appeals to reflection we have examined all make substantive empirical assumptions about the reflective process, and, unfortunately, many of these substantive assumptions turn out to be mistaken. Reflecting on first-order states is not a panacea for the many difficulties to which such states are susceptible.

None of this should suggest, of course, that reflection is useless or that we should rest content with whatever our first-order states and processes happen to produce in us. Reflection may not be the cure for all that ails us, but that does not mean that it can never be of any use at all. What we need is a realistic view of the powers of reflection, a view of reflection which allows us to assess its strengths and weaknesses. As the preceding discussion has surely made clear, such a view can only be had by way of experimental work in cognitive science. The first-person perspective on our reflective powers will not reveal them for what they are.

The time is ripe, I believe, for such an assessment. The last thirty years have seen a good deal of work on this issue, and there is a picture of reflection which has begun to emerge from the experimental literature which sheds light on the topics we have discussed here. Any such assessment is, inevitably, tentative. New results continue to emerge, and any conclusions one reaches may need to be revised in light of such results. This is simply the nature of empirical work. Some philosophers worry that this holds philosophical conclusions hostage, as they see it, to the progress of empirical inquiry. But this is no more of a problem for philosophical conclusions than the fact that conclusions in chemistry or physics or biology are hostage to new results which may emerge there. Our inquiries are constrained by what we discover. The solution to this is not to ignore relevant discoveries in order to avoid such constraints.

5.1 System 1 and System 2[1]

In 1977, Walter Schneider and Richard Shiffrin published two important papers[2] which made the case for a distinction between what they called controlled and automatic processing of information. The purpose of these papers was to present a unified framework for interpreting a wide range of results in the literature on detection, search, attention, perceptual learning, and categorization. In one experiment, subjects were given a series of letters to memorize; they were allowed to take as long as they wished to memorize the letters. Subjects were then divided into two groups. One group was asked whether any of the memorized letters were present in a series of cards, each of which contained several letters. The other group was asked whether any of the memorized letters were present in a series of cards each of which contained a combination of letters and numbers. It was found that performance was considerably better in the second of these conditions. In addition, when the number of letters memorized was increased, or the number of items on the presented cards was increased, performance was impaired only slightly in the second group, but it was impaired significantly in the first group. Schneider and Shiffrin therefore suggested that two different processes were at work in the two conditions, and they devised a series of experiments both to test and to refine that hypothesis. In the end, they came to the conclusion that there were indeed two fundamentally different sorts of processes at work here. One of these is extremely demanding of cognitive resources, requires attention, involves serial processing, and operates under the subject's control. The other is highly efficient, does not require attention, involves parallel processing, and operates without any control on the part of the subject. The first of these two processes was labelled 'controlled'; the second, 'automatic'. As Schneider and Shiffrin argued, this distinction not only made sense of the many experiments they themselves performed; it made sense of a good deal of work in the wider literature.

---

[1] I am indebted in this section to the historical account of the development of the distinction between System 1 and System 2 given by Frankish and Evans in their paper, 'The Duality of Mind: An Historical Perspective', in Jonathan St. B. T. Evans and Keith Frankish (eds), *In Two Minds: Dual Processes and Beyond* (Oxford University Press, 2009), 1–29.

[2] Schneider and Shiffrin, 'Controlled and Automatic Human Information Processing I: Detection, Search and Attention', *Psychological Review*, 84 (1977), 1–66, and Shiffrin and Schneider, 'Controlled and Automatic Human Information Processing II: Perceptual Learning, Automatic Attending and a General Theory', *Psychological Review*, 84 (1977), 127–89.

Arthur Reber's work on implicit learning was conducted entirely independently of the work of Schneider and Shiffrin; indeed, Reber's 1993 book[3] on the topic does not even mention their papers. The burden of Reber's work was to establish a distinction between two fundamentally different kinds of learning processes, which he labelled explicit and implicit. Implicit processes, whose operation he documented in experiments involving a variety of artificially constructed grammars, operate in a manner which is unavailable to introspection. While subjects learned to abide by the rules of the various artificial grammars, recognizing whether strings conformed or failed to conform to grammatical rules, they were unable to state the rules to which grammatical strings conformed. This contrasts, of course, with explicit learning of rules, which may either occur when the rules are taught directly, or by way of self-conscious theorizing. Reber argued[4] that implicit learning differs along a number of significant dimensions from explicit learning: (1) while explicit learning is subject to a variety of disorders, implicit learning remains largely intact in the face of these disorders; (2) while the quality of explicit learning tends to vary with age, implicit learning is largely independent of age; (3) the quality of explicit learning varies a great deal across individuals, while the quality of implicit learning does not; (4) much of implicit learning is common across species, while the various processes involved in explicit learning are not. Reber further argued that many of the mechanisms of implicit learning are evolutionarily older than those of explicit learning. Although there are obvious parallels here with Fodor's work on the modularity of mind,[5] Reber distances himself[6] from Fodor's work for reasons that we need not go into here. It is clear in retrospect, however, even if it was not clear at the time, that Reber was making a number of suggestions which bear some important similarities to the proposal of Schneider and Shiffrin.

Two process accounts also appear in the literature on reasoning. Nisbett and Wilson's important paper of 1977[7] made it quite clear that while many

[3] Reber, *Implicit Learning and Tacit Knowledge: An Essay on the Cognitive Unconscious* (Oxford University Press, 1993).

[4] Ibid. 88.

[5] Jerry Fodor, *The Modularity of Mind: An Essay on Faculty Psychology* (MIT Press, 1983).

[6] See especially Reber, *Implicit Learning and Tacit Knowledge*, 6.

[7] Richard Nisbett and Timothy Wilson, 'Telling More Than We Can Know: Verbal Reports on Mental Processes', *Psychological Review*, 84 (1977), 231–59. See also Wilson, *Strangers to Ourselves: Discovering the Adaptive Unconscious* (Harvard University Press, 2002).

beliefs are formed by way of processes whose workings are entirely unavailable to conscious reflection, this is not to say that we do not form beliefs about the manner in which such beliefs are formed. Instead, as they found, reflection on the manner in which our beliefs are formed may, in a wide range of circumstances, lead to entirely erroneous beliefs about the source of our first-order states. The beliefs formed when reflecting may thus involve confabulation; in such cases, second-order beliefs are largely epiphenomal with respect to the first-order beliefs whose origins they misrepresent. This is not to say, of course, that all second-order belief is a matter of confabulation, or that all second-order belief is epiphenomenal with respect to first-order states.

Work by Evans and Over,[8] in part under the influence of Reber's ideas, studied the differences between explicit and implicit reasoning, that is, cases where rules of inference are, and those where they are not, self-consciously formulated and followed. Explicit reasoning, they argued, is carried out in an independent, and more recently evolved, cognitive system, one unique to humans. It is slower than the system involved in implicit reasoning, and far more demanding of cognitive resources.

The terminology of System 1 and System 2, which is now very widely used, was introduced by Keith Stanovich.[9] As Stanovich pointed out, a large number of theorists seemed to be triangulating in on quite similar views across a wide range of cognitive processes. Stanovich himself was most directly interested in differences in reasoning across individuals, and he found that there were certain cognitive processes which showed great variability between individuals, while others did not. This difference in variability, however, proved not to be an isolated phenomenon. Rather, it seemed to go along with several other important dimensions of difference. Processes which are part of what is now called System 1 are not only typically low in variation across individuals, they are also fast, involve parallel processing, are unavailable to introspection, automatic,

---

[8] Jonathan St. B. T. Evans and David Over, *Rationality and Reasoning* (Psychology Press, 1996). See also Evans, *Hypothetical Thinking: Dual Processes in Reasoning and Judgement* (Psychology Press, 2007).

[9] See Keith Stanovich, *Who is Rational? Studies of Individual Differences in Reasoning* (Lawrence Erlbaum, 1999), and the more recent *The Robot's Rebellion: Finding Meaning in the Age of Darwin* (University of Chicago Press, 2004), as well as his 'Individual Differences in Reasoning and the Algorithmic/Intentional Level Distinction in Cognitive Science', in Adler and Rips (2008: 414–36).

evolutionarily older, and tend to be found in species other than humans. Processes which are part of System 2 vary significantly across individuals, are slow, involve serial processing, are present to consciousness, subject to control, evolutionarily more recent, and tend to be found only in humans. This clustering of characteristics is evidence that the division of mental mechanism into System 1 and System 2 is nothing shallow or arbitrary, but rather a deep and important difference constituting psychological natural kinds.[10]

We need to be cautious in bringing the literature on System 1 and System 2 to bear on the topic of reflection and the various philosophical debates which are the focus of this book. There are, of course, questions about the strength of the evidence in favor of this distinction. Addressing these questions is complicated by the fact that the many psychologists who endorse this distinction, or who argue in favor of what they call a dual process view, often use quite different terminology to refer to what appear to be quite similar phenomena, or use the same or similar terminology to refer to what are quite clearly different phenomena.[11] Sorting all of this out is highly non-trivial. In addition, it is important that one not simply identify the processes of System 2 with the kind of reflection which is the subject matter of this book. While System 2 is often the source of second-order belief, not all of the beliefs produced by System 2 are second-order, and thus when psychologists speak of System 2 as involved in reflection, their use of that term better accords with everyday usage, which allows that we may reflect on various features of the world around us and not just on features of our mental life, than it does with the technical usage here which ties reflection to second-order states. As will become clear below, talk of control in this literature is not to be taken at

---

[10] I have presented and defended a conception of natural kinds which ties it to homeostatically clustered features in *Inductive Inference and its Natural Ground* (MIT Press, 1993), chs. 2 and 3. This notion of natural kinds was first introduced by Richard Boyd in 'How to Be a Moral Realist', in Geoffrey Sayre-McCord (ed.), *Essays on Moral Realism* (Cornell University Press, 1988), 181–228, and 'Realism, Anti-Foundationalism and the Enthusiasm for Natural Kinds', *Philosophical Studies*, 61 (1991), 127–48. Richard Samuels defends this interpretation of the distinction between System 1 and System 2 in 'The Magical Number Two, Plus or Minus: Dual-Process Theory as a Theory of Cognitive Kinds', in Evans and Frankish (2009: 130–46). See also Frankish, 'Systems and Levels: Dual-System Theories and the Personal-Subpersonal Distinction', in Evans and Frankish (2009: 96).

[11] Stanovich addresses some of these differences quite directly in 'Individual Differences in Reasoning and the Algorithmic/Intentional Level Distinction in Cognitive Science'.

face value either, and the connection between so-called controlled psychological processes and agency will need to be sorted out.

None of these difficulties, however, should be seen as providing reason for turning away from this body of literature. It is clearly relevant, in some cases quite directly relevant, to the issues addressed in the first four chapters of this book. If we wish to sort through those issues, and get a clear handle on our best available theories of the phenomena at issue, we will need to work through the literature on System 1 and System 2. So let us turn to that task.

5.2 System 2 and reflection

Evans and Over see System 2 as characterized by 'conscious reflective thought'.[12] Stanovich sometimes refers to part of System 2 as 'the reflective mind'.[13] Mercier and Sperber refer to the kinds of reasoning and decision making characteristic of System 2 as involving 'reflective inferences'.[14] Carruthers remarks that one might be tempted to think of System 2 as divided into

three distinct sub-components . . . : one charged with conscious, reflective, belief-fixation; one subserving conscious, reflective, goal-adoption; and one of which takes conscious decisions (thereby formulating new intentions) in the light of one's conscious beliefs and goals.[15]

One could easily get the impression that System 2 has a great deal to do with reflection. It is important to recognize, however, that the way in which these theorists use the term 'reflection' is quite different from the way in which I have used that term in this book, and, indeed, the way in which philosophers have typically used that term.

When these theorists speak of 'conscious, reflective thought', the term 'reflective' is redundant. They mean to say nothing more than that the kind of thought characteristic of System 2 is conscious. For example, the

[12] Evans and Over, *Rationality and Reasoning*, 154.
[13] See e.g. Stanovich, 'Distinguishing the Reflective, Algorithmic, and Autonomous Minds: Is it Time for Tri-Process Theory?', in Evans and Frankish (2009: 57).
[14] Hugo Mercier and Dan Sperber, 'Intuitive and Reflective Inferences', in Evans and Frankish (2009: 149–70).
[15] Peter Carruthers, 'An Architecture for Dual Reasoning', in Evans and Frankish (2009: 110). In the end, Carruthers does not endorse this view of System 2.

application of rules in System 1 does not involve consciously entertaining any rules, and, indeed, need not involve any beliefs about rules. When theorists speak of the application of rules in System 2, however, they are referring to a process which involves bringing rules to consciousness; this will typically involve beliefs about rules. Talk of inference in System 1 does not involve conscious activity of any sort. Talk of inference in System 2, however, involves bringing thoughts to consciousness. None of this, however, amounts to the claim that System 2 inevitably brings with it anything second-order.[16] The thoughts which are brought to consciousness in System 2 need not be thoughts about the thinker's mental states.

Consider a simple example. Someone who knows that a certain conditional is true—if p, then q—and who then comes to learn that the antecedent is true, will often come to believe that the consequent of the conditional is true as well. This inference may be performed automatically by System 1 without any thoughts about the conditional statement, or its antecedent, or its consequent being brought to consciousness. The entire inferential process may take place without any conscious attention. At times, however, inferences like this may occur as a result of the focus of conscious attention. Someone carefully working out the consequences of their beliefs, for example, may consciously entertain the thought that p, together with the thought that if p then q, and then may consciously come to believe that q. The conscious thoughts entertained by such a person might include the thought that this inferential transition is valid, but, of course, that thought need not pass through such a person's mind. Similarly, one might reach the conclusion that q in a different way. One might first consciously think about the content of one's beliefs. One might consciously reflect on the fact that one believes that p, and one also believes that if p then q, and this might lead one to consciously entertain the thought that one should, therefore, believe that q. When one's inference is carried out using System 2, what is essential is that thoughts constitutive of the inference occur consciously. It is not essential, however, that these thoughts be about one's own mental states.

---

[16] Obviously, those who accept a higher-order theory of consciousness will want to insist that conscious thought is automatically second-order. My point here is simply that the distinction between System 1 and System 2 does not, by itself, bring such a commitment with it.

By the same token, the automatic processing which goes on in System 1 need not lack second-order content. An agent may make inferences about his or her own mental states without focusing attention on these inferences; such processes may occur without bringing any beliefs to consciousness.

One further point about System 2 deserves special emphasis. We should be careful to recognize that we cannot simply assume that whenever a series of propositions passes through the conscious mind, even when such a series is accompanied by some feeling of endorsement of the last of the propositions, or endorsement of the last on the basis of the earlier ones, that this amounts to belief on the basis of reasoning.[17] Believing a proposition to be true should not be identified with having it pass before one's mind consciously while accompanied by some feeling of endorsement. A belief is a representational state which is embedded in one's cognitive economy in a particular way. Among other things, it must be causally linked to other states in such a way that it is apt for the production of behavior in a characteristic way. Giving a precise functional characterization of just what a belief is goes far beyond the subject matter of this book. It should be sufficient to note here, however, that feelings of endorsing a proposition as true may, in many cases, come apart from genuine belief. Cases of self-deception are ones where one has a strong feeling of endorsement in propositions which one does not believe, and cases of after-the-fact rationalization or confabulation (which were discussed in section 1.3 above) involve genuine belief, but do not involve processes of conscious reasoning to a belief. What seems like belief from the first-person perspective, and what seems like reasoning from the first-person perspective, need not actually constitute belief or reasoning. When we examine the workings of System 2, then, it will be important to keep in mind that states which seem like beliefs to the agent who has them, and processes which seem like reasoning or belief acquisition to the agent who undergoes them, should not all be taken at face value.

5.3 Interactions between System 1 and System 2

Talk of two different systems for processing information should not lead one to think of these systems as functioning in ways which are entirely

---

[17] Wittgenstein makes a similar point in *Philosophical Investigations*, although, obviously, he does not put this in terms of System 1 and System 2.

independent of one another. Indeed, there can be no question whatsoever that there are interactions between System 1 and System 2; the contents of each system may play a role in the information processing which goes on in the other.

Thus, consider the way in which information is processed in System 2, the home of conscious reasoning. Let us take a paradigm case of System 2 reasoning. Suppose that Mary has misplaced her car keys. In getting ready to leave her house, she looks in her purse, where she usually leaves them, and discovers that they are not there. She then engages in a process of self-conscious reasoning, that is, the kind of reasoning which goes on in System 2. When did I last use my car keys, she asks herself, and what did I do with the keys when I last arrived home? As she consciously raises these questions, she mentally rehearses the path she followed from her car to the house, focusing her attention, at each point, on what she might have done with the keys. A number of possibilities then occur to her: she may have dropped them on her way in from the garage; she may have left them on the kitchen table when she brought in the mail; she may have taken them upstairs to the bedroom when she went to change her clothes. Having self-consciously arrived at these different possibilities, she proceeds to check each of the locations until she discovers the whereabouts of her keys.

As Mary thinks through these possibilities, a series of discrete thoughts pass through her conscious mind. But it is perfectly clear that the conscious contents of her mind cannot exhaust what goes on in her reasoning. Mary does not self-consciously entertain the thought that her keys cannot travel discontinuously through space and time. She believes this, of course, and the fact that she believes it plays a role in her reasoning: she could not possibly narrow the scope of her search in the way she does were it not for her recognition that physical objects like her keys cannot move about in such a way. This belief about the way in which physical objects move through space and time thus influences her reasoning even without being brought consciously to mind. And this is just to say that its influence takes place via System 1, rather than System 2.

Mary not only fails to self-consciously consider the possibility of discontinuous motion, she fails to self-consciously consider more homely possibilities as well. She might have simply left her keys in the car, but Mary doesn't stop to think about this possibility, not because she is careless in her thinking, but simply because, given her own habits, this is just too unlikely to bear thinking about. But again, this is just to say that the course of Mary's self-conscious reasoning is influenced by processes taking place in System 1, rather than System 2 alone.

The kind of reasoning Mary engages in is extremely common, and it inevitably involves self-consciously considering some possibilities while many others are never brought to mind. There is a cognitive explanation, however, for why many of these other possibilities are not entertained: Mary has sufficient background knowledge to show that many of these possibilities are either definitively ruled out or are extremely unlikely. Background knowledge is thus brought to bear on Mary's thinking, without being brought before her conscious mind. So System 1 plays an active role in determining the thoughts which are brought to consciousness in System 2. System 2 could not function in any useful way without System 1 playing such a role.

The examples discussed thus far involve non-deductive reasoning, and cases like this inevitably involve System 1 because a large body of background belief plays a role in such reasoning, and not all of the relevant beliefs can possibly be brought to consciousness. Background beliefs thus function behind the scenes, as it were, and the locus of such behind the scenes reasoning is System 1. This may make it tempting to think that System 2 may act without any input from System 1 when an agent reasons self-consciously from premises to a conclusion which those premises deductively entail. Even here, however, System 1 plays a crucial role in inference.

Thus, consider an agent who comes to form a belief as a result of self-consciously noticing that it follows deductively from other beliefs he holds. Suppose that Frank takes note of the fact that he believes that p and that he believes that if p then q, and he also makes note of the fact that p together with if p then q entails q. This leads him to believe that q. As Gilbert Harman has long emphasized, we should not think of this bit of reasoning as a case of deductive inference. Indeed, as Harman argues, there is no such thing as deductive inference.[18] An agent who notices, like Frank, that he holds beliefs which entail that q might reasonably come to believe that q, just as Frank does. At the same time, however, another agent who notices that he holds beliefs which entail that q might

[18] Gilbert Harman, *Thought* (Princeton University Press, 1973), ch. 10.

reasonably come to reject one of the beliefs which entail it. If q is not unreasonable in light of the agent's background beliefs, then acceptance of q is the likely upshot of noticing that it is entailed by other beliefs. If, on the other hand, q is unreasonable in the light of the agent's other beliefs, the agent is more likely to reject at least one of the beliefs required for its derivation. In neither case, then, is the agent's conclusion—whether it is acceptance of q or rejection of either p or if p then q—a simple matter of deduction.[19] As we saw in the earlier examples, however, when a large body of background beliefs play a role in determining what an agent believes, System 1 is inevitably involved. Reasoning in System 2 is thus influenced by reasoning in System 1.

While System 2 does not inevitably influence every bit of System 1 reasoning, it is nevertheless true that reasoning in System 2 may come to influence processes of reasoning in System 1. Thus, consider the beginning logic student who does not recognize that not (p or q) is equivalent to not-p and not-q. As the semester proceeds, the equivalence of these two statements becomes clear to him. He self-consciously rehearses the reasons for the equivalence, and focuses on these very reasons as he self-consciously works his way through a number of proofs. After a good deal of practice, he finds that it is no longer necessary to think about the reasons for believing these statements to be equivalent. When he sees one of these statements on a line of a proof, he is able to recognize, without thinking about it, that the other statement may be written on a later line. The equivalence of the two expressions becomes internalized: what at first had to be self-consciously rehearsed becomes automatic. But this is just to say that reasoning which was originally carried on in System 2 has now been carried over to System 1. While System 1 frequently operates in a way which is entirely independent of System 2, it nevertheless can, at times, be influenced by reasoning which goes on there.

The claim that there are two different systems of reasoning thus should not be understood to amount to the suggestion that these systems are entirely autonomous. Reasoning in System 1 may be affected by what goes on in System 2. And reasoning in System 2 is, in every case, influenced by System 1.

---

[19] Gilbert Harman has long emphasized this point. As he puts it: there is no such thing as deductive inference.

5.4 Control and automaticity

Schneider and Schiffrin's talk of automatic (System 1) and controlled (System 2) processes leads us back, inevitably, to the topic of epistemic agency. System 1 processes give rise to belief in a way which clearly involves no agency whatsoever. Belief formation of this sort is a pervasive feature of our cognitive lives. System 2 processes—which are 'controlled'—are important as well, and it is here that one may be tempted by the idea that epistemic agency is at work. Indeed, one might well think that the psychological literature on System 1 and System 2 provides empirical support for the commonsense idea that many epistemologists find attractive, which is the suggestion that there is genuine epistemic agency. For this reason, it will be worth revisiting the discussion of Chapter 3 to see how it fares in light of our understanding of System 1 and System 2.

Reasoning in System 2 is controlled in a way that reasoning in System 1 is not. Reasoning in System 1 is entirely automatic. It is triggered by external stimuli—for example, when one comes to believe that there is a table in front of one merely as a product of seeing it—rather than being initiated by some voluntary choice. Reasoning in System 2, on the other hand, may be initiated by a decision. Thus, for example, one may decide to re-evaluate one's evidence for a belief long held, or to self-consciously consider whether one ought to believe a certain controversial claim about which one has yet to reach a conclusion. However, we need to be careful not to exaggerate the difference here between System 1 and System 2, especially because claims about epistemic agency are quite hard to get a handle on.

Thus, as pointed out in Chapter 3, voluntary acts may provide input to System 1 reasoning, and, indeed, this is an utterly routine part of cognition. I voluntarily turn my head to get a look at the source of some provocative sound—some noise out in the street beneath my window, for example—and the result of this is that I am provided with important input which then, by way of System 1, serves to inform my body of beliefs. All of this takes place, in many cases, without any thought passing before my conscious mind about what I hope to accomplish by turning my head. Nevertheless, I do turn my head voluntarily, and my voluntary activity initiates a chain of reasoning in System 1. Those who wish to defend some account of epistemic agency are unanimous in viewing cases like this as ones which do not involve genuine epistemic agency.[20]

How are such cases different then from what goes on in System 2 reasoning, the kind of reasoning which Schneider and Schiffrin refer to as 'controlled', and which may seem to provide the very paradigm of epistemic agency? As noted earlier, such reasoning is typically initiated by a decision to focus one's attention on some issue or some bit of evidence. I may thus decide to think about what I should believe about the likelihood of life on other planets or, prompted by some new poll, I might think about whether this new information should lead me to revise my best estimate of my favored candidate's chances in the upcoming election. In these cases, I voluntarily focus my attention, and this initiates a process of reasoning, in this case, in System 2.

Thus far, the parallels between the two kinds of case seem far more significant than their differences. In both System 1 and System 2 reasoning, processes of reasoning may be initiated by voluntary acts. While the actions which initiate reasoning in both cases may be entirely voluntary, these actions are not acts of forming beliefs. They are, instead, actions which then provide input to belief-forming processes. And if this is sufficient for failing to regard such reasoning in System 1 as an instance of epistemic agency, then it seems that we should equally regard such cases of reasoning in System 2 as failing to provide us with instances of epistemic agency.

When I focus my attention, for example, on the latest public opinion poll in order to inform my judgment about the likely outcome of next month's election, a number of different outcomes are possible. It may be, if, for example, the results overwhelmingly favor one of the candidates, that I simply discover that I am forced to a certain conclusion straightaway, with no intervening reasoning making itself felt to my conscious mind. Cases like this, of course, most closely resemble the case of turning my head to look at the noise outside my window. And for that very reason, these cases are not the ones which make talk of epistemic agency most tempting. But I need not find that the evidence I focus on immediately leads me to draw some conclusion. Instead, the implications of the new evidence I focus on may leave me, at least initially, uncertain of what to believe. It is in these cases that we are inclined to speak of an

---

[20] See the sources cited in Ch. 3.

agent as deliberating about what to believe, and, as we saw in Chapter 3, it is here that many philosophers are inclined to see epistemic agency at work.

So let us look at cases of deliberation more carefully. We have already noted that the first step in deliberating, namely, the focusing of one's attention, no more involves epistemic agency than does the turning of one's head. And even when one focuses on a bit of evidence and fails to find oneself forced to an opinion which would constitute the end of one's inquiry, the act of focusing on a bit of evidence does tend to produce other beliefs. For example, one might initially conclude that the evidence of the latest poll, while obviously relevant to one's inquiry, is difficult to evaluate, and further thought will be required if one is reasonably to arrive at a view about the likely winner in the coming election. If one did arrive at such a belief, then this would likely prompt still further thoughts about available evidence, and still further attempts to bring it to bear on the question one ultimately seeks to answer. But this intermediate conclusion—that the new evidence is difficult to evaluate—was itself not freely chosen and the manner in which it was arrived at no more constitutes a case of epistemic agency than the case in which one finds that the evidence compels one to believe that a certain candidate will inevitably win. The conclusion that the evidence is difficult to evaluate is itself an example of belief passively formed; one finds oneself believing it after a certain amount of focusing on the evidence provided by the latest poll. There is, in such a case, no act of believing; there are simply processes at work which, when provided with certain input, passively produce particular beliefs.

So what happens next after finding oneself, at least initially, unable to resolve the question at issue? One may focus on other relevant evidence, and, here again, this may either lead to a simple resolution of the issue— where one finds oneself compelled to a certain conclusion—or, instead, compelled to conclude that one is not yet in a position to bring one's inquiry to an end. However many times such acts are repeated, there is no case here to be made for epistemic agency, and for just the reasons we have already discussed. If one such sequence does not constitute genuine epistemic agency, then repetitions of these sorts of sequences do not constitute genuine epistemic agency either.

But deliberation may take a somewhat different turn. One need not simply focus one's attention on successive bits of evidence until one finds oneself coming to a conclusion. One may, instead, self-consciously apply some sort of rule for bringing the inquiry to a resolution. Thus, in the case of the latest public opinion poll, one may decide to use some sort of formula to aggregate the evidence one has, perhaps weighting the results of different opinion polls by their track records in previous elections. In such a case, one may take out pencil and paper and calculate a result, or use some sort of statistical package available on one's computer, or calculate the results, if one is sufficiently agile, all in one's head. Cases like this seem importantly different from the cases in which one merely focuses one's attention on the evidence and then lets the evidence do its work.

But to what extent are the cases in which one self-consciously employs a rule genuinely different—at least as regards epistemic agency—from cases in which the mere focusing of attention on evidence produces a belief? First, let us consider the selection of a rule to employ to reach a conclusion. Sometimes, the effect of focusing on one's evidential situation is that a rule for resolving the issue is immediately brought to consciousness, and it is immediately obvious that this very rule is just what is needed to bring one's inquiry to a successful end. In such a case, the reasoning involving the rule is carried out by way of System 2, but the selection of the rule itself, which does not take place by way of self-conscious scrutiny of alternatives, takes place in System 1. The selection of the rule occurs passively in such cases. There may also be cases in which a question is self-consciously raised about which of a number of rules to employ. Even here, however, when the choice among the rules considered occurs by way of System 2, the rules among which one chooses are themselves produced by System 1. One thus comes to focus attention on a particular rule from among a list of options which was itself passively produced. Alternatively, one may deliberate even about the list of candidate rules, self-consciously considering which rules are worthy of more detailed consideration. But as we have already seen, no matter how much one consciously deliberates, there is always a good deal of cognitive work being done away from consciousness, and this work is being done—passively—by System 1. So the cognitive work involved in focusing on a rule to resolve one's inquiry will involve a cooperative effort between System 1 and System 2.

How does this bear on the question of whether, or to what extent, genuine epistemic agency is involved here? No one is tempted to see epistemic agency at work in the operation of System 1 processes at least in part because they operate in ways of which we are entirely unaware. Reasoning occurs in us, but in these cases, there is no temptation to suggest that we are agents with respect to that reasoning. In cases where System 2 is involved, however, we are not only aware of the reasoning occurring. After all, I may be aware that my arm is rising—for example, in a case where someone is lifting it—without in any way being tempted by the thought that I am raising my arm. So what is it aside from the mere fact that we are conscious of the reasoning going on in us that makes System 2 reasoning, at a minimum, appear to be something that we do? Why does reasoning in System 2, at least in the typical case, not even seem remotely like the case of being aware that someone is lifting one's arm?

Action is often accompanied by what Carl Ginet calls an 'actish phenomenological quality'.[21] There is simply the strong feeling, however difficult it may be to describe, that what is going on—whether it is a mental event or a bit of behavior—is one's own doing. When someone raises my arm, the feeling of my arm going up is not accompanied by such an actish phenomenological quality; it doesn't even feel like I'm raising my arm. In the ordinary course of events, however, when I do voluntarily raise my arm, the raising of my arm simply feels voluntary. And just as bits of behavior, like raising my arm, may be accompanied by such an actish phenomenological quality, mental events may also, at times, have the same sort of accompaniment. Thus, I may sometimes just find myself daydreaming about being in Venice, or I may purposefully imagine the same thing. In the latter case, but not the former, my imagining is accompanied by the characteristic actish phenomenological quality: it feels like something I do, rather than something that is merely happening to me. The same is true of bits of reasoning: they may feel like something we do, rather than something that happens to us. In the case of many bits of reasoning carried out by System 2, the characteristic actish phenomenological quality seems to be present.

Now it seems quite clear that the presence of such a feeling is neither necessary nor sufficient for agency.[22] There is a large psychological literature on illusions of agency, that is, cases where the actish phenomenological quality, to use Ginet's terminology, is created in individuals in cases where they are, demonstrably, not acting.[23] By the same token, one may fail to

---

[21] Carl Ginet, 'Freedom, Responsibility and Agency', *Journal of Ethics*, 1 (1997), 89.

[22] Ginet disagrees; ibid. 89.

[23] See e.g. A. Sato and A. Yasuda, 'Illusion of Sense of Self-Agency: Discrepancy between the Predicted and Actual Sensory Consequences of Actions Modulates the Sense of Self-

experience such a feeling in cases where, beyond doubt, one is, in fact, the agent of a particular action.[24] We are no more immune to mistake here than we are about straightforwardly perceptual matters. The fact that one experiences a feeling of agency when reasoning thus does not definitively show that the reasoning was, indeed, a product of genuine agency. Nevertheless, one might well think that, even if illusions of agency do, at times, occur, the feeling of agency is strong prima facie evidence for the existence of agency. The mere fact that error sometimes occurs is not, by itself, reason to suspect that error occurs in every case involving the feeling of agency in reasoning.

These kinds of concerns might easily lead to the thought that this issue cannot be decided without delving quite deeply into questions about the conditions required for agency, and the notoriously difficult issues that divide compatibilists from incompatibilists. Fortunately, however, I believe that we can address the issue about reasoning without having to decide these more general questions about agency.

We have seen that reasoning which is carried out by System 2 is always influenced by System 1 as well. There can be no wholly autonomous System 2 reasoning. Even in cases where one self-consciously applies a rule to address some epistemic issue, System 1 plays a crucial role. As we have seen, System 1 may be responsible for bringing a rule to mind as the obvious means to address the problem. Or the operation of reasoning in System 1 may result in a rule being selected from among a short list of options. Or the workings of System 1 may produce the short list of options itself. Or System 1 may determine whether the result of applying some rule is simply accepted as true or, instead, viewed as a reason for rejecting one of the beliefs which helped to lead to that result. In typical cases, System 1 will play more than one of these roles. And as we have seen, no one views the operation of System 1 as involving epistemic agency. So any course of reasoning involving System 2 will inevitably involve stages of reasoning, and typically multiple such stages, which are wholly passive.

Agency, But not the Sense of Self-Ownership', *Cognition*, 94 (2005), 241–55; Shelley Taylor, *Positive Illusions: Creative Self-Deception and the Healthy Mind* (Basic Books, 1989); Shelley Taylor and Jonathan Brown, 'Illusion and Well-Being: A Social Psychological Perspective on Mental Health', *Psychological Bulletin*, 103 (1988), 193–210.

[24] See e.g. Daniel T. Gilbert, Ryan P. Brown, Elizabeth C. Pinel, and Timothy D. Wilson, 'The Illusion of External Agency', *Journal of Personality and Social Psychology*, 79 (2000), 690–700; and Sato and Yasuda, 'Illusion of Sense of Self-Agency'.

the complex mental mechanisms which realize them. There is a natural tendency to see first-order mental goings-on in mechanistic terms—to view them from the third-person point of view—but to view the processes involved in reflection, instead, from the first-person perspective. When this tendency gives rise to a view of reflective processes which is any less mechanistic than one's view of first-order processes, a mystified view of reflection is inevitable.

The first step toward mystification thus involves a perspectival shift in which first-order mental processes are viewed from the third-person point of view, but reflection is instead presented from a first-person perspective. All of the authors we have examined here make this move.

Consider discussions of knowledge and justification. The standard way of presenting skeptical problems about knowledge involves exactly this shift in perspectives. One takes the point of view of the reflective agent, like Descartes in the *First Meditation*, examining his beliefs. The reflective agent is presented as engaging in a monologue of self-examination such as this.

I typically form beliefs unreflectively, and it may well be that those beliefs are reliably formed, but, instead, those beliefs might well be formed in a terribly unreliable manner. For this very reason, I now stop to reflect in order to examine the epistemic credentials of my beliefs. By reflecting on these issues, I may attempt to determine which beliefs I ought to continue to hold, if any, and which I ought to reject or suspend judgment on.

These monologues of self-examination thus present the reflective agent from the first-person point of view. At the same time, this agent acknowledges that the reflective turn is an unusual step. Descartes, for example, remarks at the very beginning of the *First Meditiation* that he waited a long time before engaging in his reflective examination of his beliefs precisely because it involves such a substantial departure from everyday activities, activities in which his attention was focused on the world rather than on his own mental states. More than this, once one engages in this reflective first-personal investigation, one inevitably views the beliefs which one formed unreflectively in third-personal terms. One questions whether the processes which produced them were reliable, for example. One asks whether, in fact, they represent the world as it actually is. One thinks about the various ways in which belief acquisition can go wrong—and here, thinking about the way in which others make mistakes through misperception, carelessness, bias, and so on, can help to make the possibility of error particularly vivid—and this helps in allowing one to think about one's own unreflective belief from the third-person point of view. I know that others have formed beliefs in ways which were terribly unreliable or inaccurate without any awareness of their own errors, and so I recognize that, in my own unreflective moments, I might be just like them.

The shift from a first-person point of view on reflective belief acquisition to a third-person point of view on unreflective belief acquisition is aided and abetted by comparison with cognition in other animals. If one assumes that other animals lack the capacity to reflect, then the animal case seems to present a particularly pure version of what unreflective belief acquisition is like. And when we think about cognition in other animals, it is particularly natural to view it from the third-person point of view. There are, beyond doubt, complex mechanisms at work in the production of cognitive states in other animals, and there are experimental programs of research for investigating just what these mechanisms are. Unreflective belief is thereby presented from a third-person perspective, in contrast with the way in which we naturally think about reflective belief acquisition—namely, from the first-person point of view.

The same is true in discussions of reasoning. Unreflective belief acquisition is presented from a third-person point of view, sometimes by way of an examination of cognition in other animals, and this is contrasted with what goes on in the reflective case, a case which is then presented, instead, from a first-person perspective. Reasoning in the reflective case is described from the perspective of the deliberating agent, an agent who wonders just what it is that he or she ought to believe. One might describe either the unreflective case or the reflective case from a first-person or a third-person perspective. It is noteworthy, however, that those who wish to mark reflection out as somehow special, those who see reflective processes as importantly different in kind from unreflective ones, have a very strong tendency to shift their perspective from a third-person to a first-person point of view when the subject matter shifts from unreflective processes to reflective ones.

So too with many discussions about freedom and responsibility. When we think about Frankfurt's wantons, it is quite natural to view them from the third-person point of view. We think of their actions in mechanistic terms: they are pushed around by their internal states. Such creatures are then contrasted with fully fledged persons—that is, creatures with second-order beliefs, desires, and volitions—and here it is natural to take the perspective of the deliberating agent. We think of the agent surveying his various desires, trying to decide which of them he wishes to be moved by, or, to put the point slightly differently, which of them he most identifies with. Do I really wish to act on my desire for the piece of cake or, instead, on my desire to stick to a diet? Do I wish to act on my desire to take the bribe, or, instead, my desire to be an honest person? What kind of person do I wish to be? If we think about action in this way, we view the wanton from the outside, while we view the person, instead, from inside.

None of this is forced, of course. We might view the wanton from the internal perspective, or the person from a third-person perspective. Nonetheless, discussions of deliberation are often illustrated by examples in which the deliberating agent is described from the first-person perspective, while the unreflective agent is described, instead, in third-person terms.

Finally, the discussion of normativity provides us with a particularly striking example of this perspectival shift. The passage already quoted from Korsgaard illustrates this point vividly:

A lower animal's attention is fixed on the world. Its perceptions are its beliefs and its desires are its will. It is engaged in conscious activities, but it is not conscious *of* them. That is, they are not the objects of its attention. But we human animals turn our attention on to our perceptions and desires themselves, on to our own mental activities, and we are conscious *of* them. That is why we can think *about* them.

And this sets us a problem no other animal has. It is the problem of the normative. For our capacity to turn our attention on to our own mental activity is also a capacity to distance ourselves from them, and to call them into question. I perceive, and I find myself with a powerful impulse to believe. But I back up and bring that impulse into view and then I have a certain distance. Now the impulse doesn't dominate me and now I have a problem. Shall I believe? Is this perception really a *reason* to believe? I desire and I find myself with a powerful impulse to act. But I back up and bring that impulse into view and then I have a certain distance. Now the impulse doesn't dominate me and now I have a problem. Shall I act? Is this desire really a *reason* to act? The reflective mind cannot settle for perception and desire, not just as such. It needs a *reason*. Otherwise, at least as long as it reflects, it cannot commit itself or go forward.[25]

The lower animal's situation is described here in third-person terms. It has certain beliefs and desires; it has a certain will. But human animals, on the other hand, are described as distanced from these internal states, and

[25] Korsgaard, *The Sources of Normativity* (Cambridge University Press, 1992), 92–3.

now, our situation is described in first-personal terms. This switch in perspectives could just as easily have proceeded in the other direction. The lower animal's situation could have been described from the animal's own point of view, while the deliberating agent could have been viewed from the outside, in third-person terms. Alternatively, the lower animal and the human could both have been described from the same perspective, using either the first-person perspective for each kind of creature, or the third-person perspective in each case. The perspectival shift, however, comes naturally, and, for this very reason, it is easy in reading passages such as this to fail to notice that the narrative shift has even occurred.

So what? I said that this perspectival shift is the first-step toward mystifying reflection, but this is not because the shift in perspective, by itself, involves any sort of mistake. Rather, the perspectival shift, in my view, makes certain sorts of mistakes particularly easy to make. It makes it easier to see first-order processes in mechanistic terms, while viewing the process of reflection as somehow different. When reflection is thus seen as different in kind from processes that go on at the first-order level, the seemingly harmless shift in narrative perspective is transformed into substantive philosophical error.

I have said that it is possible to give an account of unreflective processes from the first-person perspective. It may seem, however, that this is not obviously so. After all, insofar as they are unreflective, doesn't it follow that there really is no first-person perspective on them at all? This doesn't follow, but there is, I think, an important grain of truth here. It doesn't follow because, to take a single example, there is something it is like to have a visual sensation, even if one is not reflecting on the sensation itself. There is thus no contradiction in asking for an account of what it is like from the first-person point of view to have a sensation which is not reflected upon. Similarly, there is no contradiction in asking what processes of belief acquisition, or reasoning, or acting are like from the first-person perspective, even in cases in which they are not themselves reflected upon. At the same time, there can be little doubt that a good deal of what goes on in belief acquisition, for example, is often unavailable to the first-person perspective, and, more than this, the entire process of unreflective belief acquisition will often fail to make its presence felt from that perspective. The same is true, of course, of unreflective reasoning and unreflective action. This does not mean that we cannot give an account of what these things are like from the first-person perspective; it just means that, since there is nothing it is like, such accounts are not very substantive or interesting.

There is an important point, however, lurking here. The fact that we are capable of acquiring beliefs unreflectively in ways which do not make their presence felt from the first-person perspective does not make it even remotely tempting to suggest that, for that very reason, there are no processes at work here at all. Obviously, unreflective belief acquisition involves complex mental mechanisms working behind the scenes. And the same is true of reasoning and action. Nevertheless, when we turn to reflective processes, it does suddenly become tempting to think of the entire process, in each of these cases, as one which is fully revealed from the first-person perspective. But this is, in the end, no more plausible in the case of reflective processes than it is in the case of unreflective ones. The first-person perspective simply leaves out a great deal—indeed, most—of what goes on in the mind. And this is no less true of reflective processes than it is of unreflective ones. As we have seen, the first-person perspective also gives us a view of what goes on in our minds which is, on the one hand, extremely vivid and psychologically compelling, but, on the other hand, at best partial, and often deeply distorted. When we treat the first-person perspective as providing us with a full and accurate account of these processes, we end up with an extremely inaccurate account of them. More than this, because so much of the work, even in reflection, is performed behind the scenes, the first-person perspective on reflective processes impedes our understanding of them and turns them into something mysterious.

Remember, for example, Ernest Sosa's characterization, as he sees it, of one crucial difference between reflective and unreflective belief acquisition: 'reflection aids agency, control of conduct by the whole person, not just by peripheral modules'.[26] Unreflective belief acquisition is characterized here from the third-person point of view; it is carried out by 'peripheral modules'. Reflection, on the other hand, is carried out by 'the whole person'. There is no doubt that when we view reflection from the first-person point of view, there is a palpable feeling of agency: what Ginet calls 'an actish phenomenological quality'. So talk of agency here, and action by the whole person, comes naturally to us when we adopt the first-person perspective.

---

[26] 'Replies', in John Greco (ed.), *Ernest Sosa and his Critics* (Blackwell, 2004), 292.

And when we do that, of course, reflective belief acquisition and unreflective belief acquisition seem different in kind. But we could, just as easily,
have adopted a third-person perspective on reflective belief acquisition,
examining the System 1 and System 2 processes which come into play,
and, were we to do that, the result would have appeared to be no less
mechanistic than what goes on in the case of unreflective belief acquisition. The appearance of a difference in kind here is a product of the
different perspectives which Sosa adopts—a first-person perspective on
reflective processes, in contrast to a third-person perspective on unreflective processes—rather than a difference in the processes of belief
acquisition themselves.

I am not arguing here that talk of agency is merely an illusion. I wish to
remain neutral on questions about the relationship between mechanism
and agency. My point is simply that Sosa sees unreflective belief acquisition as 'merely' mechanical and therefore, on his view, not a product of
agency. He contrasts this with the reflective case, which he views, unlike
the unreflective case, from a first-person perspective, and now, as a result
of that perspectival shift, reflective and unreflective belief acquisition are
viewed as different in kind. The appearance of a difference in kind,
however, is due to nothing in the processes themselves; it is due entirely
to the shift from the third-person to the first-person perspective. It is here
that we move from a harmless narrative device to substantive philosophical
error.

Notice that it is the very same error which gives rise to the idea, which
we see in Laurence BonJour's work, not only that the 'core notion of
epistemic justification' involves epistemic responsibility, but that issues of
such responsibility only arise when we engage in reflection.[27] BonJour's
idea is that unreflective belief acquisition is something that merely happens
to us, not something that we do. It is, therefore, not something that we are
responsible for. The very possibility of responsible belief acquisition only
emerges when we stop to reflect, and, therefore, it is only here that talk of
epistemic justification, and thus knowledge, is appropriate. But why is it
that we should see reflective and unreflective belief acquisition as different
in this way? BonJour is quite clear about this. Such issues need to be
addressed from the agent's 'own perspective rather than from one which

---

[27] See e.g. BonJour, *The Structure of Empirical Knowledge* (Harvard University Press, 1985), 8.

unavailable to him'.[28] But, as we have seen, it is a mistake to think that these issues can be properly addressed from such a first-person point of view. The first-person perspective both leaves out and distorts crucial features of our mental life. It is only from this distorted point of view that reflective and unreflective processes seem to be different in kind.

John McDowell's work shows how this problem manifests itself on a larger stage, bringing into play not only questions about reasoning, but also issues involving understanding and the very possibility of having beliefs. Indeed, those philosophers who view these issues in terms of the Sellarsian contrast between 'the space of reasons' and the 'space of causes' illustrate very clearly how reflection can take on mystical properties. Unreflective cognitive processes—or mere information processing—takes place in 'the space of causes' while reflection occurs, instead, in the 'space of reasons'. This characterization, of course, nicely encapsulates the perspectival shift I have been focusing on. Unreflective processes are naturally viewed from a third-person perspective, and so we see them in mechanistic terms: inhabitants of the space of causes. But when we view reflective processes, instead, from the first-person point of view, we now view our internal states, not as states which are causally related to one another, or as states which bear nomological relations to one another, but, instead, as ones which may serve as reasons for one another: they thereby leave the space of causes and enter the space of reasons. The space of reasons thus becomes a mysterious realm, one which occupies a place devoid of event-causal and nomological connections. There is, of course, no such place. The temptation to believe in it only emerges as a product of the perspectival shift.

The same mistake occurs in the literature on freedom of the will. As noted earlier, Frankfurt remarks that the wanton—the creature who lacks second-order beliefs, desires, and volitions—is 'a helpless bystander to the forces that move him'.[29] This is supposed to contrast with the situation of what Frankfurt regards as a genuine person—a creature with the full range of second-order states. But if one's worry about wantons is that they are merely pushed around by their internal states, the fact that persons have a wider array of such states will surely fail to address one's concern. Once again, we see a certain mechanistic view of the mental economy

---

[28] Ibid. 44.

[29] Harry Frankfurt, 'Freedom of the Will and the Concept of a Person', repr. in *The Importance of What we Care about: Philosophical Essays* (Cambridge University Press, 1988), 21.

of first-order states, but then, as a result of a first-person presentation of the reflective agent, a view of persons which presupposes that second-order states work in some other way. There is, however, no reason to think that the mental economy of second-order states is different in kind from that of first-order states. The supposition that reflection is different in kind from first-order mentality presents us with a picture of a free-floating agent, picking and choosing among a variety of first-order mental states. While this may accurately portray how things seem when we deliberate, it offers us a thoroughly mysterious account of the workings of reflection. Instead of explaining how reflection actually works, this picture offers us little more than an account of how things seem from the first-person point of view masquerading as an explanation.

Attempts to give an account of normativity which link it to reflection constitutively similarly depend on mystification. We have examined a number of different attempts to provide this linkage. On one view, examination of the world around us can only result in descriptions, and so we need to turn to something else—reflection—if we are to produce the prescriptions which are the key to normativity. Any such argument founders when it comes up against the need to explain how reflection could produce anything but descriptions either. Perhaps it is mysterious how empirical investigation could ground normative claims. It is, however, no less mysterious how reflection could do so. The mystery of the former does not in any way do away with the mystery of the latter. Embracing an account of normativity in terms of features of reflection simply accepts one mystery instead of another. Nor does it help to suggest that such an account may be secured by recognizing that normative demands must have their origin in features of the self rather than features of the world outside us. Even if that were correct, we would have to endow reflection with powers it simply does not have to suppose that it can be counted upon to get at the relevant features of the self. The hard work involved in understanding the sources of normativity cannot be shortcircuited by assigning magical powers to the processes involved in reflection.

The problematic accounts of reflection which allow it to function in a way which is different in kind from first-order processes has its origin in the perspectival shift, a shift from a third-person perspective on first-order processes to a first-person perspective on reflection. The real error arises, however, when the shift to the first-person perspective is taken to give us a full and accurate account of reflective processes. The first-person perspective cannot do this. The accounts of reflection which emerge when one supposes that it can lead to mystification rather than insight.

5.6 Conclusion

The processes involved in reflection have long seemed utterly different from those which are involved in unreflective mental processes. These apparent differences have influenced philosophical views about a very wide range of topics. In this book, we have examined four such topics: knowledge, reasons, freedom, and normativity. In each case, we have seen that some apparently commonsensical ideas about the importance of reflection lead to an infinite regress. They lead to the view that knowledge, reasoning, freedom, and normativity are impossibilities. This is not at all what philosophers who have stressed the importance, and the specialness, of reflection have intended. But even when the infinite regress is somehow avoided, we have seen that the processes of reflection are endowed by these philosophers with properties they could not possibly possess. Reflection is thereby mystified, its special place assured not by understanding it, but by a failure to see it for what it is.

The processes involved in reflection are, to be sure, different in some ways from those involved in unreflective processes. The mystification of reflection arises, however, from seeing it as different in a particular way. First-order mental processes are seen as mechanical, while reflective processes are not. First-order processes are viewed as things which happen to us; second-order processes are seen as a product of our agency. First-order processes are seen as ones which operate outside of consciousness; second-order processes are seen as wholly present to introspection. None of these contrasts, however, is accurate.

The temptation to see reflection in this way arises from the utter naturalness of viewing unreflective processes from a third-person perspective, while viewing reflective processes from a first-person perspective. When the shift in perspective is not recognized, the processes themselves may seem different in the ways enumerated in the last paragraph. These apparent differences, however, are not due to real differences in the processes themselves. They are due, instead, to the shift in perspective. It is thus crucial, if we are to see reflection aright, that we do not make such misleading comparisons. If we are to understand reflection for what it is, we must examine it from the third-person perspective.

The literature on System 1 and System 2 is useful in precisely this way. The workings of reflection are seen as no less mechanical than the workings of unreflective mental processes. They are no more a product of agency than unreflective processes. And, just as with unreflective processes, they are not always accurately or fully revealed for what they are by introspection. When viewed in this way, the processes involved in reflection are thereby demystified.

Human beings are different from other animals in quite a number of ways, and our ability to reflect on our mental states may, perhaps, be one of those differences. It is important, however, not to exaggerate what such a difference would amount to. The important project of self-understanding is not advanced by mystification. As we come to understand more about the mechanisms of reflection, we will have a better understanding of what it is and isn't good for. Such an understanding can only come about as a great deal more detail emerges from the empirical literature. At this point, there are no easy or sweeping conclusions. That unexciting conclusion, however, may be all that can be hoped for if we are to appreciate reflective processes for what they are.

Bibliography

Adler, Jonathan, and Rips, Lance (eds), *Reasoning: Studies of Human Inference and its Foundations* (Cambridge: Cambridge University Press, 2008).

Alcock, John, *Animal Behavior: An Evolutionary Approach*, 8th edn. (Sunderland, Mass.: Sinauer Associates, 2005).

Allen, Colin, and Bekoff, Marc, *Species of Mind: The Philosophy and Biology of Cognitive Ethology* (Cambridge, Mass.: MIT Press, 1997).

Alston, William, 'Two Types of Foundationalism', *Journal of Philosophy*, 73 (1976), 165–85.

——'The Deontological Conception of Epistemic Justification', *Philosophical Perspectives*, 2 (1988), 257–99.

American Psychiatric Association, *Diagnostic and Statistical Manual of Mental Disorders (DSM-IV)*, 4th edn. (Washington, DC: American Psychiatric Association, 1994).

Arpaly, Nomy, *Unprincipled Virtue: An Inquiry into Moral Agency* (Oxford: Oxford University Press, 2003).

——*Merit, Meaning, and Human Bondage: An Essay on Free Will* (Princeton: Princeton University Press, 2006).

Astington, Janet Wilde, *The Child's Discovery of the Mind* (Cambridge, Mass.: Harvard University Press, 1993).

——Harris, Paul, and Olson, David (eds), *Developing Theories of Mind* (Cambridge: Cambridge University Press, 1988).

Baker, Lynne Rudder, 'Moral Responsibility without Libertarianism', *Noûs*, 40 (2006), 307–30.

Bargh, J. A., Chen, M., and Burrows, L., 'Automaticity of Social Behavior: Direct Effects of Trait Construct and Stereotype Activation on Action', *Journal of Personality and Social Psychology*, 71 (1996), 230–44.

Bender, John (ed.), *The Current State of the Coherence Theory: Critical Essays on the Epistemic Theories of Keith Lehrer and Laurence BonJour, with Replies* (Dordrecht: Kluwer, 1989).

Bennett, Jonathan, 'The Conscience of Huck Finn', *Philosophy*, 49 (1974), 123–34.

Bermúdez, José Luis, *Thinking without Words* (Oxford: Oxford University Press, 2003).

——'Knowledge, Naturalism and Cognitive Ethology: Kornblith's *Knowledge and its Place in Nature*', *Philosophical Studies*, 127 (2006), 317–35.

Bishop, Michael, 'In Praise of Epistemic Irresponsibility: How Lazy and Ignorant Can You Be?', *Synthese*, 122 (2000), 179–208.

BonJour, Laurence, *The Structure of Empirical Knowledge* (Cambridge, Mass.: Harvard University Press, 1985).

——'The Indispensibility of Internalism', *Philosophical Topics*, 29 (2001), 47–65.

——'Kornblith on Knowledge and Epistemology', *Philosophical Studies*, 127 (2006), 317–35.

Boyd, Richard, 'How to Be a Moral Realist', in Geoffrey Sayre-McCord (ed.), *Essays on Moral Realism* (Ithaca, NY: Cornell University Press, 1988), 181–228.

——'Realism, Anti-Foundationalism and the Enthusiasm for Natural Kinds', *Philosophical Studies*, 61 (1991), 127–48.

Brandom, Robert, *Making it Explicit: Reasoning, Representing and Discursive Commitment* (Cambridge, Mass.: Harvard University Press, 1994).

——*Articulating Reasons: An Introduction to Inferentialism* (Cambridge, Mass.: Harvard University Press, 2000).

——*Between Saying and Doing: Towards an Analytic Pragmatism* (Oxford: Oxford University Press, 2008).

——*Reason in Philosophy: Animating Ideas* (Cambridge, Mass.: Harvard University Press, 2009).

Byrne, Richard, 'Social and Technical Forms of Primate Intelligence', in F. de Waal (ed.), *Tree of Origin: What Primate Behavior Can Tell Us about Human Social Evolution* (Cambridge, Mass.: Harvard University Press, 2001), 145–72.

Carroll, Lewis, 'What the Tortoise Said to Achilles', *Mind*, 4 (1895), 278–80.

Carruthers, Peter, 'An Architecture for Dual Reasoning', in Evans and Frankish (2009: 109–27).

——*The Opacity of Mind: An Integrative Theory of Self-Knowledge* (Oxford: Oxford University Press, 2011).

Cheney, Dorothy, and Seyfarth, Robert, *How Monkeys See the World: Inside the Mind of Another Species* (Chicago: University of Chicago Press, 1990).

Chomsky, Noam, *Syntactic Structures* (The Hague: Mouton, 1957).

——*Aspects of the Theory of Syntax* (Cambridge, Mass.: MIT Press, 1965).

Christensen, David, 'Conservatism in Epistemology', *Noûs*, 28 (1994), 69–89.

Cohen, G. A., *If You're an Egalitarian, How Come You're So Rich?* (Cambridge, Mass.: Harvard University Press, 2001).

Conee, Earl, and Feldman, Richard, *Evidentialism: Essays in Epistemology* (Oxford: Oxford University Press, 2004).

Davidson, Donald, 'Thought and Talk', repr. in *Inquiries into Truth and Interpretation* (Oxford: Oxford University Press, 1984), 155–70.

——'Rational Animals', repr. in *Subjective, Intersubjective, Objective* (Oxford: Oxford University Press, 2001), 95–105.

Dennett, Daniel, *Brainstorms: Philosophical Essays on Mind and Psychology* (Montgomery, Vt.: Bradford Books, 1978).

——*Elbow Room: The Varieties of Free Will Worth Wanting* (Cambridge, Mass.: MIT Press, 1984).

DeSousa, Ronald, *Why Think?* (Oxford: Oxford University Press, 2007).

Devine, P. G., 'Stereotypes and Prejudice: Their Automatic and Controlled Components', *Journal of Personality and Social Psychology*, 56 (1989), 5–18.

Epley, Nicholas, and Gilovich, Thomas, 'When Effortful Thinking Influences Judgmental Anchoring: Differential Effects of Forewarning and Incentives on Self-Generated and Externally Provided Anchors', *Journal of Behavioral Decision Making*, 18 (2005), 199–212.

Ericsson, K. Anders, and Simon, Herbert, *Protocol Analysis: Verbal Reports as Data*, revised edn. (Cambridge, Mass.: MIT Press, 1993).

Evans, H. E., *The Comparative Ethology of the Sand Wasps* (Cambridge, Mass.: Harvard University Press, 1966).

Evans, Jonathan St. B. T., *Bias in Reasoning: Causes and Consequences* (Hillsdale, NJ: Lawrence Erlbaum, 1989).

——*Hypothetical Thinking: Dual Processes in Reasoning and Judgement* (Hove: Psychology Press, 2007).

——*Thinking Twice: Two Minds in One Brain* (Oxford: Oxford University Press, 2010).

——and Frankish, Keith (eds), *In Two Minds: Dual Processes and Beyond* (Oxford: Oxford University Press, 2009).

——and Over, David, *Rationality and Reasoning* (Hove: Psychology Press, 1996).

Fairweather, Abrol, and Zagzebski, Linda (eds), *Virtue Epistemology: Essays on Epistemic Virtue and Responsibility* (Oxford: Oxford University Press, 2001).

Fehrman, Kenneth, and Fehrman, Cherie, *Color: The Secret Influence*, 2nd edn. (Upper Saddle River, NJ: Prentice-Hall, 2003).

Feldman, Richard, 'Epistemic Obligations', *Philosophical Perspectives*, 2 (1988), 235–56.

——'The Ethics of Belief', *Philosophy and Phenomenological Research*, 60 (2000), 667–95.

——'Voluntary Belief and Epistemic Evaluation', in Steup (2001: 77–92).

——'Chisholm's Internalism and its Consequences', *Metaphilosophy*, 34 (2003), 603–20.

Fodor, Jerry, *The Modularity of Mind: An Essay on Faculty Psychology* (Cambridge, Mass.: MIT Press, 1983).

Foley, Richard, 'What am I to Believe?', in Steven Wagner and Richard Warner (eds), *Naturalism: A Critical Appraisal* (Notre Dame, Ind.: University of Notre Dame Press, 1993), 147–62.

Frank, Michael, and Smith, Crystal, 'Illusion of Control and Gambling in Children', *Journal of Gambling Studies*, 5 (1989), 127–36.

Frankfurt, Harry, 'Freedom of the Will and the Concept of a Person', repr. in *The Importance of What We Care About: Philosophical Essays* (Cambridge: Cambridge University Press, 1988), 11–25.

——*Necessity, Volition, and Love* (Cambridge: Cambridge University Press, 1999).

Frankish, Keith, *Mind and Supermind* (Cambridge: Cambridge University Press, 2004).

——'Systems and Levels: Dual-System Theories and the Personal-Subpersonal Distinction', in Evans and Frankish (2009: 89–107).

——and Evans, Jonathan St. B. T., 'The Duality of Mind: An Historical Perspective', in Evans and Frankish (2009: 1–29).

Garnham, Alan, and Oakhill, Jane, *Thinking and Reasoning* (Oxford: Blackwell, 1994).

Garrett, J., and Brooks, C., 'Effect of Ballot Color, Sex of Candidate, and Sex of College Students of Voting Age on their Voting Behavior', *Psychological Reports*, 60 (1987), 39–44.

Gilbert, Daniel T., Brown, Ryan P., Pinel, Elizabeth C., and Wilson, Timothy D., 'The Illusion of External Agency', *Journal of Personality and Social Psychology*, 79 (2000), 690–700.

Gilovich, Thomas, Griffin, Dale, and Kahneman, Daniel (eds), *Heuristics and Biases: The Psychology of Human Judgment* (Cambridge: Cambridge University Press, 2002).

Ginet, Carl, 'Freedom, Responsibility and Agency', *Journal of Ethics*, 1 (1997), 85–98.

——'Deciding to Believe', in Steup (2001: 63–76).

Goodman, Nelson, *Fact, Fiction, and Forecast*, 3rd edn. (Indianopolis: Bobbs-Merrill, 1973).

Gopnik, Alison, 'How We Know Our Minds: The Illusion of First-Person Knowledge of Intentionality', *Behavioral and Brain Sciences*, 16 (1993), 1–15 and 90–101.

——and Meltzoff, Andrew, *Words, Thoughts and Theories* (Cambridge, Mass.: MIT Press, 1997).

Greco, John (ed.), *Ernest Sosa and his Critics* (Oxford: Blackwell, 2004).

Halberstadt, Jamin, and Wilson, Timothy, 'Reflections on Conscious Reflection: Mechanisms of Impairment by Reasons Analysis', in Adler and Rips (2008: 548–65).

Hampshire, Stuart, *Freedom of the Individual* (London: Chatto & Windus, 1965).

Harman, Gilbert, *Thought* (Princeton: Princeton University Press, 1973).

——*The Nature of Morality: An Introduction to Ethics* (Oxford: Oxford University Press, 1977).

Haugeland, John, *Having Thought: Essays in the Metaphysics of Mind* (Cambridge, Mass.: Harvard University Press, 1998).

Hauser, Marc, *The Evolution of Communication* (Cambridge, Mass.: MIT Press, 1996).

——Cushman, Fiery, Young, Liane, Jin, R. Kang-Xing, and Mikhail, John, 'A Dissociation between Moral Judgments and Justifications', *Mind and Language*, 22 (2007), 1–21.

Heil, John, 'Doxastic Agency', *Philosophical Studies*, 43 (1983), 355–64.

——'Doxastic Incontinence', *Mind*, 93 (1984), 56–70.

Johnson-Laird, Philip, *How We Reason* (Oxford: Oxford University Press, 2006).

Jones, Karen, 'Emotion, Weakness of Will, and the Normative Conception of Agency', in Anthony Hatzimoysis (ed.), *Philosophy and the Emotions* (Cambridge: Cambridge University Press, 2003), 181–200.

Kahneman, Daniel, Slovic, Paul, and Tversky, Amos (eds), *Judgment under Uncertainty: Heuristics and Biases* (Cambridge: Cambridge University Press, 1982).

Kane, Robert, *The Significance of Free Will* (Oxford: Oxford University Press, 1996).

Kelley, Darcy, 'Vocal Communication in Frogs', *Current Opinion in Neurobiology*, 14 (2004), 751–7.

Kornblith, Hilary, 'Introspection and Misdirection', *Australasian Journal of Philosophy*, 67 (1989), 410–22.

——'The Unattainability of Coherence', in Bender (1989: 207–14).

——*Inductive Inference and its Natural Ground* (Cambridge, Mass.: MIT Press, 1993).

——'The Impurity of Reason', *Pacific Philosophical Quarterly*, 81 (2000), 67–89.

——'Epistemic Obligation and the Possibility of Internalism', in Fairweather and Zagzebski (2001: 231–48).

——*Knowledge and its Place in Nature* (Oxford: Oxford University Press, 2002).

——'Sosa on Human and Animal Knowledge', in Greco (2004: 126–34).

——'The Metaphysical Status of Knowledge', *Philosophical Issues*, 17 (2007), 145–64.

——'Sosa in Perspective', *Philosophical Studies*, 144 (2009), 127–36.

——'Reasons, Naturalism, and Transcendental Philosophy', in P. Sullivan and J. Smith (eds), *Transcendental Philosophy and Naturalism* (Oxford: Oxford University Press, forthcoming).

Korsgaard, Christine, *The Sources of Normativity* (Cambridge: Cambridge University Press, 1996).

——*The Constitution of Agency: Essays on Practical Reason and Moral Psychology* (Oxford: Oxford University Press, 2008).

——*Self-Constitution: Agency, Identity, and Integrity* (Oxford: Oxford University Press, 2009).

Kunda, Ziva, *Social Cognition: Making Sense of People* (Cambridge, Mass.: MIT Press, 1999).

Lackey, Jennifer, 'Why We Don't Deserve Credit for Everything We Know', *Synthese*, 158 (2007), 345–61.

Lehrer, Keith, *Metamind* (Oxford: Oxford University Press, 1990).

Lettvin, J. Y., Maturana, H. R., McCulloch, W. S., and Pitts, W. H., 'What the Frog's Eye Tells the Frog's Brain', repr. in Warren McCulloch, *Embodiments of Mind* (Cambridge, Mass.: MIT Press, 1965), 230–55.

Lucas, E. J., and Ball, L. J., 'Think-Aloud Protocols and the Selection Task: Evidence for Relevance Effects and Rationalisation Processes', *Thinking and Reasoning*, 11 (2005), 35–66.

McDowell, John, *Mind and World (With a New Introduction by the Author)* (Cambridge, Mass.: Harvard University Press, 1996).

Mackie, J. L., *Ethics: Inventing Right and Wrong* (Harmondsworth: Penguin, 1977).

Mallon, Ron, 'Social Roles, Social Construction and Stability', in Frederick F. Schmitt (ed.), *Socializing Metaphysics: The Nature of Social Reality* (Lanham, Md.: Rowman & Littlefield, 2003), 327–53.

Marr, David, *Vision* (W. H. Freeman, 1982).

Mercier, Hugo, and Sperber, Dan, 'Intuitive and Reflective Inferences', in Evans and Frankish (2009: 149–70).

Merikle, P. M., 'Perception without Awareness: Critical Issues', *American Psychologist*, 47 (1992), 792–5.

Moran, Richard, *Authority and Estrangement: An Essay on Self-Knowledge* (Princeton: Princeton University Press, 2001).

Nagel, Thomas, *Mortal Questions* (Cambridge: Cambridge University Press, 1979).

—— *The View From Nowhere* (Oxford: Oxford University Press, 1986).

Nisbett, Richard, and Ross, Lee, *Human Inference: Strategies and Shortcomings of Social Judgment* (Upper Saddle River, NJ: Prentice-Hall, 1980).

—— and Wilson, Timothy, 'Telling More than We Can Know: Verbal Reports on Mental Processes', *Psychological Review*, 84 (1977), 231–59.

Pauer-Studer, Herlinde (ed.), *Constructions of Practical Reason: Interviews on Moral and Political Philosophy* (Stanford, Calif.: Stanford University Press, 2002).

Pereboom, Derk, *Living without Free Will* (Cambridge: Cambridge University Press, 2001).

Pinker, Steven, 'Language Acquisition', in Lila Gleitman and Mark Liberman (eds), *An Invitation to Cognitive Science*, i, 2nd edn. (Cambridge, Mass.: MIT Press, 1995), 135–82.

Plantinga, Alvin, *Warrant: The Current Debate* (Oxford: Oxford University Press, 1993).

Povinelli, Daniel, *Folk Physics for Apes: The Chimpanzee's Theory of How the World Works* (Oxford: Oxford University Press, 2000).

—— and Eddy, T. J., 'What Young Chimpanzees Know about Seeing', *Monographs of the Society for Research in Child Development*, 61 (1996), 1–152.

Quine, W. V. O., 'Natural Kinds', in *Ontological Relativity and Other Essays* (New York: Columbia University Press, 1969), 26–68.

Reader, Simon, and Laland, Kevin (eds), *Animal Innovation* (Oxford: Oxford University Press, 2003).

Reber, Arthur S., *Implicit Learning and Tacit Knowledge: An Essay on the Cognitive Unconscious* (Oxford: Oxford University Press, 1993).

Ristau, Carolyn, 'Aspects of the Cognitive Ethology of an Injury-Feigning Bird, the Piping Plover', in Carolyn Ristau (ed), *Cognitive Ethology: The Minds of Other Animals* (Hillsdale, NJ: Lawrence Erlbaum Associates, 1991), 91–126.

Roush, Sherrilyn, 'Second Guessing: A Self-Help Manual', *Episteme*, forthcoming.

Rubinoff, M., and Marsh, D., 'Candidates and Color: An Investigation', *Perceptual and Motor Skills*, 50 (1980), 868–70.

Ryan, Sharon, 'Doxastic Compatibilism and the Ethics of Belief', *Philosophical Studies*, 114 (2003), 47–79.

Samuels, Richard, 'The Magical Number Two, Plus or Minus: Dual-Process Theory as a Theory of Cognitive Kinds', in Evans and Frankish (2009: 130–46).

Sato, A., and Yasuda, A., 'Illusion of Sense of Self-Agency: Discrepancy between the Predicted and Actual Sensory Consequences of Actions Modulates the Sense of Self-Agency, But Not the Sense of Self-Ownership', *Cognition*, 94 (2005), 241–55.

Schantz, Richard (ed), *The Externalist Challenge* (Berlin and New York: de Gruyter, 2004).

Schneider, Walter, and Shiffrin, Richard M., 'Controlled and Automatic Human Information Processing I: Detection, Search and Attention', *Psychological Review*, 84 (1977), 1–66.

Schwitzgebel, Eric, 'The Unreliability of Naive Introspection', *Philosophical Review*, 117 (2008), 245–73.

Sellars, Wilfrid, *Science, Perception, and Reality* (London: Routledge & Kegan Paul, 1963).

Shettleworth, Sara, *Cognition, Evolution and Behavior* (Oxford: Oxford University Press, 1998).

Shiffrin, Richard M., and Schneider, Walter, 'Controlled and Automatic Human Information Processing II: Perceptual Learning, Automatic Attending and a General Theory', *Psychological Review*, 84 (1977), 127–89.

Shoemaker, Sydney, 'On Knowing One's Own Mind', repr. in *The First-Person Perspective and Other Essays* (Cambridge: Cambridge University Press, 1996), 25–49.

——'Self-Intimation and Second-Order Belief', *Erkenntnis*, 71 (2009), 35–51.

Skinner, B. F., and Ferster, Charles, *Schedules of Reinforcement* (New York: Appleton Century Crofts, 1957).

Sloman, Steven, 'Two Systems of Reasoning', in Gilovich *et al.* (2002: 379–96).

Smith, Eliot, and Miller, Frederick, 'Limits on Perception of Cognitive Processes: A Reply to Nisbett and Wilson', *Psychological Review*, 85 (1978), 355–62.

Sosa, Ernest, 'Knowledge and Intellectual Virtue', repr. in *Knowledge in Perspective: Selected Essays in Epistemology* (Cambridge: Cambridge University Press, 1991), 225–44.

——'Reflective Knowledge in the Best Circles', *Journal of Philosophy*, 94 (1997), 410–30.

Sosa, Ernest, 'Replies', in Greco (2004: 275–325).

—— 'Two False Dichotomies: Foundationalism/Coherentism and Internalism/ Externalism', in W. Sinnott-Armstrong (ed.), *Pyrrhonian Skepticism* (Oxford: Oxford University Press, 2004), 146–60.

—— *A Virtue Epistemology: Apt Belief and Reflective Knowledge*, i (Oxford: Oxford University Press, 2007).

—— *Reflective Knowledge: Apt Belief and Reflective Knowledge*, ii (Oxford: Oxford University Press, 2009).

—— 'Replies to Commentators on *A Virtue Epistemology*', *Philosophical Studies*, 144 (2009), 137–47.

—— *Knowing Full Well* (Princeton: Princeton University Press, 2011).

Stanovich, Keith, *Who is Rational? Studies of Individual Differences in Reasoning* (Hillsdale, NJ: Lawrence Erlbaum, 1999).

—— *The Robot's Rebellion: Finding Meaning in the Age of Darwin* (Chicago: University of Chicago Press, 2004).

—— 'Individual Differences in Reasoning and the Algorithmic/Intentional Level Distinction in Cognitive Science', in Adler and Rips (2008: 414–36).

—— 'Distinguishing the Reflective, Algorithmic, and Autonomous Minds: Is it Time for Tri-Process Theory?', in Evans and Frankish (2009: 55–88).

—— *Rationality and the Reflective Mind* (Oxford: Oxford University Press, 2011).

Sterelny, Kim, *The Evolution of Agency and Other Essays* (Cambridge: Cambridge University Press, 2001).

—— *Thought in a Hostile World: The Evolution of Human Cognition* (Oxford: Blackwell, 2003).

Steup, Matthias (ed.), *Knowledge, Truth, and Duty* (Oxford: Oxford University Press, 2001).

—— 'Doxastic Freedom', *Synthese*, 161 (2008), 375–92.

Taylor, Shelley, *Positive Illusions: Creative Self-Deception and the Healthy Mind* (New York: Basic Books, 1989).

—— and Brown, Jonathan, 'Illusion and Well-Being: A Social Psychological Perspective on Mental Health', *Psychological Bulletin*, 103 (1988), 193–210.

Tiberius, Valerie, *The Reflective Life: Living Wisely with Our Limits* (Oxford: Oxford University Press, 2008).

Tomasello, Michael, 'Chimpanzees Understand Psychological States: The Question is Which Ones and to What Extent', *Trends in Cognitive Science*, 7 (2003), 153–6.

—— and Call, Josep, *Primate Cognition* (Oxford: Oxford University Press, 1997).

Tversky, Amos, and Kahneman, Daniel, 'Judgment under Uncertainty: Heuristics and Biases', *Science*, 185 (1974), 1124–31.

Vauclair, Jacques, *Animal Cognition: An Introduction to Modern Comparative Psychology* (Cambridge, Mass.: Harvard University Press, 1996).

Wason, Peter, and Evans, Jonathan St. B. T., 'Dual Processing in Reasoning', *Cognition*, 3 (1975), 141–54.

Watson, Gary, 'Free Agency', *Journal of Philosophy*, 72 (1975), 205–20.

Williams, Michael, 'Is Knowledge a Natural Phenomenon?', in Schantz (2004: 193–210).

Wilson, Timothy, *Strangers to Ourselves: Discovering the Adaptive Unconscious* (Cambridge, Mass.: Harvard University Press, 2002).

——and Nisbett, Richard, 'The Accuracy of Verbal Reports about the Effects of Stimuli on Evaluations and Behavior', *Social Psychology*, 41 (1978), 118–31.

Wooldridge, Dean, *The Machinery of the Brain* (New York: McGraw Hill, 1963).

Unlike the case in which someone raises one's arm—where one is aware that one's arm is being raised—these workings of System 1 operate in ways of which one is typically unaware. The result is that one has an awareness of the operations of System 2, and yet, despite the fact that much of what occurs is being dictated by System 1, it feels, from the inside, as if all of one's reasoning is taking place before one's conscious mind. And this is just to say that the ways in which System 2 interacts with System 1 produce an illusion that one is fully aware, and in full control of, the actual course of one's reasoning. Far from showing that System 2 reasoning involves epistemic agency of a sort which cannot be found in reasoning produced by System 1, an understanding of the operations of System 2 and its interaction with System 1 thus serves to show how an illusion of control is produced whenever System 2 goes to work.

The philosophers we have been discussing argue that while there is no epistemic agency involved in first-order belief acquisition, belief acquisition involving reflection—that is, belief acquisition involving beliefs about one's own beliefs—crucially involves epistemic agency. I have not taken any stand here on whether genuine epistemic agency exists. What I have argued, however, is that there is no basis for the view that reflection involves a kind of agency that does not exist without it. Reflection on the content of one's beliefs, their source, and the logical relations among them does tend to lead to an illusion of a kind and degree of control that one does not have in the absence of reflection, and it is precisely this illusion which makes the claim that reflection and agency are linked appear so plausible. But in the final analysis, there is no reason to believe that the distinction between reflective and unreflective belief acquisition tracks the distinction between beliefs which are a product of epistemic agency and those which are merely arrived at passively. A fortiori, there is no reason to assign any special status to beliefs reflectively arrived at—for example, that we are uniquely responsible for these beliefs—in virtue of alleged differences in agency.

5.5 Reflection without a free-floating agent

The key to a demystified view of reflection is the recognition that, just as first-order mental processes are realized in complex mental mechanisms, we can only understand second-order mental processes by understanding

Index